SCHOOLWISE

Schoolwise
Teaching Academic Patterns of Mind

Joan Estes Barickman

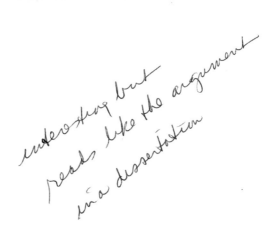

interesting but
reads like the argument
in a dissertation

Boynton/Cook
HEINEMANN
Portsmouth, NH

Boynton/Cook Publishers
A Subsidiary of
Heinemann Educational Books
361 Hanover Street
Portsmouth, NH 03801

Offices and agents around the world

Copyright © 1992 by Joan Estes Barickman

Library of Congress Cataloging in Publication Data

Barickman, Joan Estes.
    Schoolwise : teaching academic patterns of mind / Joan Estes
Barickman.
        p. cm.
    Includes bibliographical references.
    ISBN 0-86709-309-9
    1. Learning—Research. 2. Learning, Psychology of—Research.
    3. Thought and thinking—Research. 4. Action research in education.
    I. Title.
LB1060.B38 1992
370.15'23—dc20   92-22088
                                                             CIP

Cover design by Tom Allen
Printed in the United States of America on acid-free paper
92 93 94 95 96 9 8 7 6 5 4 3 2 1

Contents

*p. 64 and ff —
good WAC
activities*

Preface

I started thinking about thought three days after I entered a new elementary school. My first day, a gang of girls chased me all the way home, teasing and threatening me. The next day, in the playground, I told the gang leader I'd "twist her neck into a pretzel." The third day, I found myself sitting outside the fifth-grade classroom at the "bad boys" table during lunch and recess. I was out there many more days.

I learned to love Jamey at that table. Every recess, we sat there together in the long, two-tone grey, silent hall. Everything we said was hushed and crucial. We shared our deepest thoughts. He told me that "hell was a state of mind." I know how that sounds now, when I'm over fifty, but when we were eleven, it was profound and painful. From the school's point of view, I guess he may have been a "bad boy." From my point of view, he was brilliant, decent, and anguished. By high school, I didn't see him often. By my graduation, he'd died in an automobile accident.

Books, like everything meaningful, are driven by passion. I wanted to help Jamey then and I still, passionately, want children like him to be capable of success and happiness. My husband, Richard, has encouraged me to pursue that desire for more than thirty years. He has contributed to every page of this book. My children, Christopher and Julia, are also here. They're the only people, besides my husband, who have let me see their thoughts develop day by day over many years.

My students' minds are also represented here in *Schoolwise.* I've rearranged details so that, with two exceptions, particular students and situations aren't identifiable. Every quote is accurate, even though the names are changed. I've used two students' actual names. Those two had already publicly distributed writing I wanted to quote. All of the personal traits, ideas, feelings, and attitudes I describe are real. I appreciate all of those many students who shared their thoughts with me, even when those thoughts were painful.

Chapter One

Fearsome and Glorious
Introduction

I'm driving to work. Suddenly, the car dies. I pump the gas, flip the key on and off, and then wait, hoping it's simply flooded. Finally, helpless, I call the Scarpo Brothers' Garage.

Sometimes teaching seems the same. When students stop learning, we try a few hit-or-miss techniques, but don't really know what's wrong. What's the connection between teaching and learning? How does the mind work?

There's certainly interest in finding out. In 1981, *Educational Leadership* devoted an issue to thinking and learning. In the many years since, educators have focused on teaching thinking more and more. Districts hire consultants in "thinking skills," set up thinking skills committees, and adopt thinking skills programs. Both the teachers' unions and the Association for Supervision and Curriculum Development have thinking skills networks; and there are international conferences about teaching thinking. There was even a national project in Venezuela to increase intelligence in the populace.

We yearn for a Scarpo Brothers to call to our classrooms. According to the National Institute of Education, we've had a revolution in cognitive studies as important to learning theory as Einstein's research was to physics or Darwin's to biology. However, we can't depend on science or social science to find out how children think and learn; no matter how much we've discussed these outside cognitive theories in our committees and networks since 1981, they haven't helped much in our classrooms.

In fact, Western philosophers investigated thought for 2500 years before modern cognitive science. Philosophers have certainly given

1

us the metaphors that govern our everyday notions of what the mind is: a reasoning device, a blank slate, a developing plant, an animal to train, or an intellectual athlete. Aristotle, Locke, Rousseau, Bentham, and Dewey provide us a context for our everyday decisions, but they certainly don't specify the workings of the mind. While their metaphors have influenced the general sort of schools we have, the free schools based on Rousseau, for example, or the comprehensive schools based on Bentham, they don't help us make consistent minute-to-minute classroom choices.

Someday maybe neuroscientists will be able to show how neurons, axons, and synapses actually create thought. Yet despite a great deal of activity in genetics, biochemistry, and neurophysiology, neuroscientists still can't agree on how our billions of brain cells actually work together to think. Their research certainly can't apply to pedagogy yet. So far, it doesn't help my teaching to know that education enlarges a rat's brain or that acetylcholine affects memory. Yet our leaders and our committees mistakenly turn theories like the triune brain, the left and right brains, and brain growth spurts into educational practice. Several years ago, I heard serious suggestions that eleven-year-old children stop attending school and work for three years because they were between brain growth spurts. Proposals like that one are dangerous to children and offensive to most teachers.

When neuroscientists try to understand thinking, they observe the brain; psychologists and sociologists infer thinking from human behavior; that's all they can see. The early psychologists tested intelligence; they identified and invented mental activities like "synthesizing" simply by the test items they chose. Developmental psychologists like Bruner, Erikson, Gesell, Freud, and Piaget meticulously describe behavior seemingly characteristic of certain "stages" and make hypotheses about what thought structures might produce such behavior. But "assimilation" and "accommodation" do not really explain any physical activity of the mind. Hofstader and others involved in artificial intelligence try to isolate characteristics of intellect by simulating thought on computers, but so far computers cannot approach the complexity of even a child's mind. Basil Bernstein, Michael Cole, and other sociologists speculate by observing the interaction of people and their environment. Finally, sociolinguists and psycholinguists like Chomsky and Vygotsky analyze language patterns and hypothesize intellectual structures which either cause or result from language development. Comparatively little of this psychological or sociological research is directed toward actual children learning and actual teachers teaching.

School is a special environment. It's not just about the physical development of the brain. It's more complex than the psychologist's laboratory; it's more condensed and intentional than other communities studied by sociologists. School is a place where wisdom too great for any one person is shared with young people who, not always willingly, must reconceive it. That one interaction condenses virtually every other aspect of culture into a moment we call learning. That moment, which is largely internal, can be understood best by people who participate in it. It can only be "observed" by people who have known thousands of such moments. Teachers are able to observe the daily interactions of a class or to note successful long-term learning in individual students who return to visit at their twenty-fifth reunions. Virtually no published research is done by elementary and secondary classroom teachers; yet these teachers and students are the only people who can look at that moment both from without and within, from the present and the past.

Philosophers, scientists, and social scientists have many suggestive theories. Naturally we need to use their ideas to inform our own observations. Why, though, do we simply study their research? Why do we stop short of making our own inferences? Who should do research about the relation of teaching and thinking? Those of us who deal year in and year out with developing minds in learning situations. Then, when our teaching stalls, we'll know better what to do.

Good teachers are always researchers, of course, in our day-to-day hypotheses, tests, and revisions. My "sense" of what works is, like the "intuitions" of many other teachers, an unarticulated hypothesis tested over thirty years of teaching. Every individual student is a tiny research project. Right now we are the best researchers to clarify the crucial relationship among thinking, learning, and teaching and to develop effective ways to change children's minds.

Politics and economy are as important to developing pedagogy as neuroscience and social science. As part of a cultural system, we have limited options. We are restricted by the state, the district, the building, and the department, as well as by our own needs and those of our students. Bus schedules and administrators' personalities often have as much influence on class procedures as cognitive theories. How often can we actually develop methods based on Bruner or Bloom anyway? How consistently do districts allow experimentation with effective school research or learning styles theories? Every teacher must constantly negotiate a settlement (often brilliant) which gets the most from what's possible. Who is best qualified to understand how these restrictions influence teaching and learning? We can develop methods that take account of them. We change the system slowly by changing ourselves. There are a few systemic changes afoot—sparked by the Coalition of Essential Schools and a variety of alternative schools—but most of us must work within the system we have.

We must work together. Sometimes we forget that even though we don't get the high salaries paid in other professions, we get the highest sign of respect: parents give us their children. We share a trust and a mission. Bertrand Russell describes what we teach—thought— as fearsome and glorious: "Men fear thought as they fear nothing else on earth—more than ruin—more even than death. . . . Thought looks into the pit of hell and is not afraid. Thought is great and swift and free, the light of the world and the chief glory of man" (1926).

We must share whatever knowledge there is so that we may fulfill that trust. Teachers always "team teach" even though we don't usually conceive of our jobs that way. We depend on every student's previous teachers and we influence the success of each student's future teachers. Learning in my composition class depends on the content acquired in history and the logical organization practiced in science. If we are to be effective, we must be a research team. We must have common goals; and we must have a common vocabulary so that we can work together to implement those goals.

Right now, college, secondary, and elementary teachers seldom talk to one another. We don't even share the same theorists. Derrida, Foucault, and Lacan are virtually unknown to high school literature teachers, though they have been important influences in college. Even in the secondary English "content area," research in the relationship of writing and thinking is a quite separate field from the relationship of reading and thinking. Reading is also quite different from literature. English is even further divided from math, science, and history.

We need our own vocabulary rather than sporadically-borrowed words from other disciplines. Philosophy, neuroscience, and medicine, as well as cognitive psychology and sociology all have distinct vocabularies. So does each subdivision of those disciplines. The meanings, for example, of "schema," "patterns," "operations," "functions," "life spaces," and "plans," as well as seemingly common words like "thinking" and "intuition," even vary from one group of cognitive psychologists to another. Teachers need to use commonplace words because our concern is "how children think and learn in school," not neurobiology or cognitive psychology or sociolinguistics. At the same time, we should not be so offended by jargon that we don't use relevant research.

Consider this book, then, a conversation among colleagues. It isn't primarily philosophy, science, or social science although they're considered. We'll try to learn from everyone who knows about teaching, thinking, and learning: lawyers, football coaches, religious leaders, therapists, advertisers, game designers, mathematicians, poets, rock musicians, and comedians. You'll find Jean Piaget, Thomas Jefferson, and René Descartes in *Schoolwise.* But you'll also find Woody Allen and Don, my custodian. This book is informed speculations that may illuminate our classroom experiences. It's also team planning. It proposes a goal, drawn from our past and present, and a simple shared vocabulary. *Schoolwise* represents research, but not the narrow behaviorist approach that has characterized educational inquiry for so long. Our research method is introspection, informed, if sceptical, observation, and eclectic, tested selection of other people's theories. We'll talk about Laura and Kimmie, two students who graduated before 1981, the date that marks such interest in thinking and learning. Are they now meeting goals set for them back then? What educational experiences improved or limited their cognitive growth?

Schoolwise doesn't pretend to explain how children think. It *does* suggest how to change their thinking. Above all it is practical. Considering how little we know about the mind (or how much we suspect), perhaps practicality is more honest and productive than any assertion of truth. Only by speculating together and using all the resources possible can teachers become the real researchers in the relationship of thinking, learning, and teaching.

Chapter Two

Besides Common Sense
Academic Thinking for
At-risk Students

At Christmastime my phone at home rang. The local police. Did I have a Christmas tree in my classroom? Yes. A blue spruce? Yes. A particularly large, magnificent blue spruce? Pretty magnificent. And were Andy McGrath and Tony Belushi in my class? Later, Andy wrote the story in Figure 2-1.

Andy isn't a thief; he just wanted to get his English teacher a Christmas tree. He is also aware, as the ironic tone and title show, that other people might understand the situation somewhat differently.

He's not a "good" student either. He finds school nearly intolerable. He can't take notes, but if he could, he wouldn't be able to decipher them. About his reading assignments, he says, "O.K., I'll do the multiple choice at the end of the chapters, but I can't remember for ten minutes." He's right. His teachers, he says, make him feel stupid. His teachers think he's not only stupid, but also lazy—and nasty besides. Last fall, when I phoned his former history teacher about his "drop" in U. S. history, she said, "No, I DON'T have to talk about Andy McGrath. I don't EVER have to talk about him again. He's not in my class anymore." And she hung up. This person, a good teacher, a good friend, and an extremely tolerant person, found Andy intolerable.

Andy simply does not think the way we want him to. Our system makes him feel stupid and us feel frustrated. Our school structure and curriculum implies a rather limited definition of thinking and

Figure 2-1

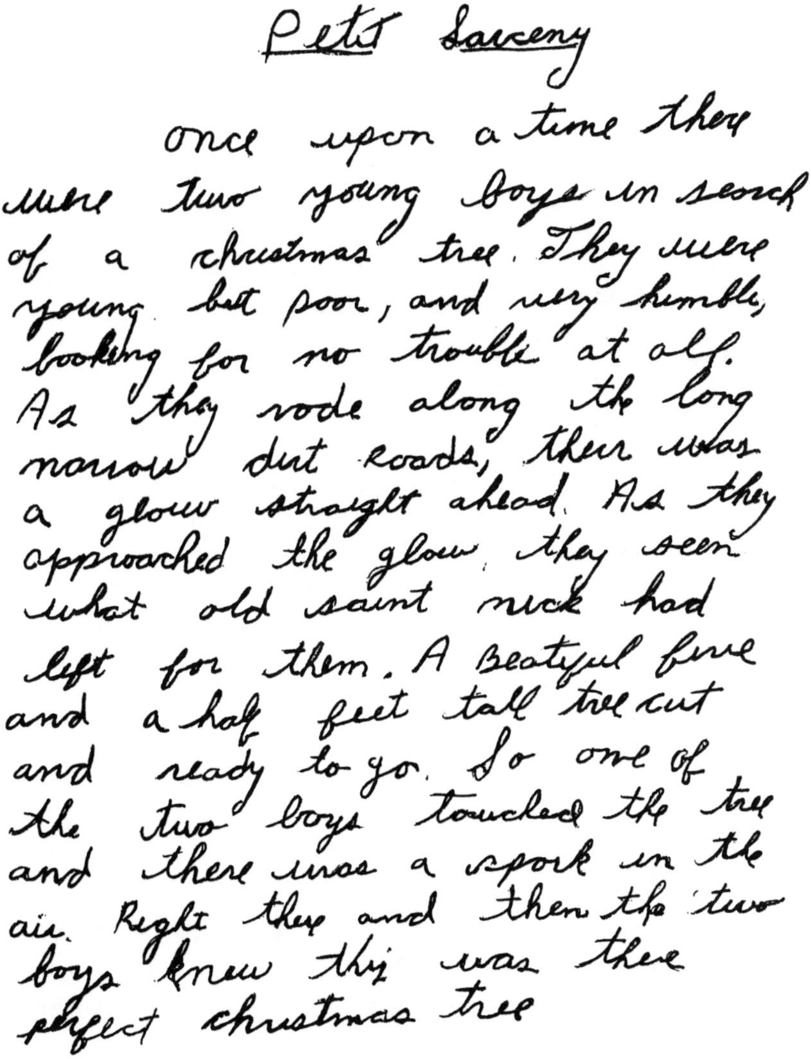

> _Petit Larceny_
>
> Once upon a time they were two young boys in search of a christmas tree. They were young but poor, and very humble, looking for no trouble at all. As they rode along the long narrow dirt roads, there was a glow straight ahead. As they approached the glow, they seen what old saint nick had left for them. A Beatyful five and a half feet tall tree cut and ready to go. So one of the two boys touched the tree and there was a spark in the air. Right then and then the two boys knew thy was there perfect christmas tree

circumscribed developmental theory: tacitly we define all "good" thinking as "scientific," "critical" thought and we believe development moves from Andy's commonsense intuitions at the lower level to some ideal student's "scientific" logic at the higher level.

We can discern our schools' belief in this definition and developmental sequence in the way we structure our teaching. In the early grades we teach experientially, in the later elementary grades with activity and words, after middle school almost entirely through reading, writing, and listening. In high school, teachers certainly assume that students understand at Bloom's comprehension stage (1956). That assumption explains the predominance of quizzes, multiple choice, and fill-in-the-blank activities. Habitually, we distribute information and presume the children will somehow understand and remember it. Sometimes it's facts—1776; sometimes it's more abstract—the salient aspects of modern Japanese economy. We don't usually deal with *how* or *why* children manage to "learn." If children don't learn, we assume they're "slow" or "*dis*affected."

We expect this development from "lower order thinking" to "higher order thinking" in concepts, attitudes, skills, and language. First of all, Andy is supposed to learn both to specify and to generalize concepts more and more as he goes through school. By high school, he should perceive and remember finer and finer distinctions; instead, for example, of understanding international politics in terms of single issues (WWI was caused by the assassination of the Archduke Francis Ferdinand or WWII by the invasion of Poland), we want him to be able to identify the precise economic, moral, religious, and political elements of each event. We also want him to generalize. When he was five, he knew that cats are more like lions than like dogs. At seventeen, we expect him to read a Renaissance play like *Romeo and Juliet* "intelligently": he has to be able to understand the period, to comprehend the ideas of drama and tragedy, and not just struggle through, but even enjoy, an unfamiliar language; most important, he must recognize all the particulars of character and plot and find meaningful analogies between the difficulties of Romeo, Juliet, Tybalt, and Mercutio and his own problems with family, friendship, love, and violence.

We also expect children to develop from ego-centric to other-centric attitudes. As he gets older, we want Andy to be conscious of places and times further and further away; as he learns about the ancient Greeks and the South Africans, we hope he will develop a sense of detachment and objectivity. Perhaps, occasionally, he will question himself and his culture: "Why do some countries have a higher mortality rate?" " Was Kennedy's decision on Cuba right?" We expect him to develop a conscious, active exercise of intellect and move from a dualistic sense of right and wrong to a relativistic contextual understanding. The development of these assumptions ("decentering," Piaget would say) about the relation of the individual to the world is, in fact, the development of Socrates' "examined" life which our Enlightenment forefathers so valued.

Schools also expect students to increase the speed, number, automaticity, and simultaneity of skills. By high school, Andy must listen, write, summarize, sort, connect, question, and restructure information simultaneously—just in routine notetaking. Much more complex skills are expected daily as he reads science and social studies assignments, analyzes literature, solves algebra problems, prepares for tests, and meets deadlines.

The development of "academic" or "analytic" language occurs along with the growth of "critical" thought. In kindergarten, children can use words with general or single meanings and sentences with simple structures. By ninth grade, they must have developed many discipline-specific vocabularies with precise meanings; they must also understand ambiguity and implication. They must learn to comprehend complex sentences and compose many forms of writing.

This developmental sequence rests on some major assumptions about what thinking is and what it is for. Most of the time, we assume that "critical reasoning" is the only definition of mature thinking. It isn't. "Scientific" reasoning is not even the primary pattern of reasoning in schools. In most schools this critical thinking is expected in science, social studies, and sometimes in literature. It is NOT expected in music, art, cooking, drama, or physical education. In fact, art and music, which require highly developed difficult patterns of thought, are often regarded as less important than the "academic" subjects. We also assume that "critical thinking" is the definition of "good" thinking. Glatthorn and Baron, for example, describe the distinction I'm making between Andy's common sense and academic reasoning as the difference between poor thinking and good thinking (Costa, 1985, 50). *It's not.* Actually, Andy's common sense is the appropriate mode of reasoning in most everyday situations.

The goal of common sense is to take action; we perceive what is necessary for that action. In ordinary life, we need to take quick action on partial information all the time. Truthfully, none of us lives a consistently rational life. Day to day, we all live in a small cognitive world. Our values come primarily from our family; our effective knowledge is limited; most of our deepest assumptions remain unquestioned. We act on our feelings and reason to justify them. "It's O.K. for my son to work off the books because rich people have tax write-offs" isn't much different from "Somebody else cut down the tree to steal it. When I found it, it was half littering the street." Common sense reduces to simple principles. Sometimes these principles are unattractive; prejudice, for example, is an ugly simplification. Sometimes these principles are essential for survival. As de Bono points out, a person simply couldn't contemplate all the variables in the thousands of situations which occur daily (1971). In fact, the newspapers, the television, and most faculty meetings tell us, with a little reflection, that Andy's common sense is, indeed, common to us all. Reasoning by common sense is as valid in some contexts as is academic reasoning (or, in fact, reasoning by faith) in others.

Andy simply carries his commonsense assumptions and patterns into the classroom. Our ideal student has developed "academic" assumptions. For him the goal of thinking is not just action, but reflection; the purpose of learning is learning. Usually his reason to learn particular information (immigration patterns in U. S. history) is so far in the future that he can't explain its value any better than "knowledge is power" or "get into college." For Andy, those explanations are nonsense. If Andy doesn't see the immediate use of information, he forgets it. For him, the whole purpose of learning is immediate action. Will it keep him out of trouble? Will it help him get a car? Since Andy's assumptions about the meaning and use of thinking are totally different from our school definitions, his attitudes, behavior, and language are quite different from what we expect.

The "academic" student sees high school as a place to play with ideas. He wants to revise his thinking. Andy comes to school already knowing the "truths" of his culture and family. He doesn't want to question values or methods. He's afraid of ambiguity and new ideas. He just wants to avoid being wrong. An "academic" wants to form judgments, Andy opinions. An "academic" wants to behave justly. Andy wants to protect himself and his friends.

Our ideal academic students value remembering and actively try to "learn." They believe that learning is hard work. When they don't understand a problem in math, they go over it several times and experiment with different strategies. They telephone each other: "Did you get number 6? How did you do it? What if you solved for x first?" For social studies, they make outlines or charts. They try to be precise—labeling, classifying, and remembering actively. After years of practicing skills, refining attitudes, and acquiring knowledge, the ideal academic student learns more and faster.

Andy does not even know that this active sorting and structuring exists in anyone's mind, much less that it is necessary. Andy thinks school learning is attending classes (and after twelve years of unhappy failure his attendance is still nearly perfect) and "doing" schoolwork (which he still "does" assiduously). If he does that, he assumes he's learning. His reading is decoding, not comprehending; his writing is copying straight out of his head or the book, not composing. He memorizes by looking at his book; he takes tests by what he remembers. Trying hard means trying the same thing again. His best work is repetition (and garbled at that) and his final, concise, accurate summary of most of his educational experience is: "This is stupid. I already learned that!"

Andy responds, when he responds, impulsively and defensively. In writing, for example, he only revises spelling and punctuation if the teacher points out errors; he cannot evaluate his text against the effect it might have on an audience because he has little sense of audience. He also says, "What? Change it how? That's what's in my head. They're *my* ideas. *You* can't make me change my ideas!" He is not, from his point of view, separate from his text at all; and writing is not a series of choices. He has similar difficulties with literature. He can't think of a novel as an artifact intentionally crafted to mean something. In global studies, he has trouble empathizing with unfamiliar cultures; if you discuss Buddhism, he is likely to think you're preaching its beliefs. Dispassionate intellectual debate isn't in his world view. He also doesn't consider multiple points of view in his everyday behavior. In social interactions as well as in the science lab, he generalizes from too few variables—the Christmas tree, for example: "I want a beautiful tree, my teacher wants a beautiful tree, it's already cut down" is quite enough information for him to take action.

Some of the greatest differences between Andy and a traditional "ideal" student occur in the way they use language. Andy expresses himself often in stories—temporal, human, and (often intricately) analogical. He has mastered the fable. If he wants to tell me something difficult, he'll start, "Once there was this chicken; it lived in a farmyard with a bunch of other chickens and a lady farmer named Farmer Barickman . . . ." The more academic student's justification for the tree would have been, had he stolen it at all, a dissertation on the need for social action in the face of the dehumanization of the modern classroom. It would have used highly embedded sentence structure, differentiated vocabulary, and references to complex ideas and systems—economy, capitalism, and exploitation.

"Critical" reasoning is not the definition of "good" thought; it is one kind of thought. We also make two other unwarranted assumptions. One of them is that we assume we have, in the United States, the correct developmental sequence; the corollary is that any cultures that think differently are inferior. It's not so. Just because a continuum appears to exist in our public schools does not mean that this development represents innate, universal, cognitive structures, applicable to all peoples. It does not mean that tribal cultures must value classification by logical class rather than function or that non-Western cultures must value detachment and objectivity as we do. It does not even mean that all people in Western culture naturally go through this development. Andy hasn't.

The next assumption is that if Andy doesn't go through this development, he simply is stupid. *He's not.* There is no evidence at all that academic reasoning ever develops from commonsense reasoning. If academic reasoning doesn't develop from commonsense reasoning, what does? How will Andy, without intervention, reason when he is forty-five? There are very few studies of adult reasoning modes. However, it is a truism that children frequently turn out like their parents. Mozart came from a musical family, John Stuart Mill from an intellectual family, and Andy from Mr. and Mrs. McGrath. There is considerable corroborating evidence from psychology and sociology that learning begins at home: children learn language, feeling, attitude, and reasoning before they are six years old.

Children get their early understanding about what information is good for from their parents. Are they uncomfortable or comfortable? Hungry or full, wet or dry, alone or together? How can they perpetuate or alter the situation? What works? What doesn't? Whatever seems successful determines their attitudes toward learning. If acquiring information, remembering, questioning, and playing with words are valued and modeled, they will likely develop those activities. People give meaning to experience by the way they order it— even little people. People order experience according to the models in their immediate culture. At home, children develop many preconceptions. Those preconceptions determine perception—how they see, smell, feel, touch, and hear. How do six-year-olds correctly recognize a "Mercedes"? They have a mental image of "car" and a more specific category of "Mercedes car"; otherwise, all cars would be undifferentiated details. In third grade, they will also be able to look at all sorts of lines and squiggles and identify the ones that are *e*'s because they have a preconception of *e*. Similarly, in third grade they will look at the great variety of experiences possible and they will choose which ones are valuable for learning. If they have no appropriate preconception of learning activities, they will not identify the right ones.

Nobody denies that Japanese children speak Japanese or that boys and girls from New Orleans do not sound as if they came from Yonkers. Sociolinguists have also studied the less obvious influences ethnic and socioeconomic background have on language and thought. Basil Bernstein (1974) claims that socioeconomic class influences people's attitudes toward language and thought. He identifies two "codes" of language/thought: a "restricted" code and an "elaborated" code. The restricted code is characterized by implied meanings and undifferentiated, general word use; it is context-bound and person-centered. The elaborated code is characterized by explicit meanings and differentiated word use; it is context-free and positional. The "middle class" code involves, of course, the language and thought processes of our schools. It is not, however, Andy's language. William Labov (1972) points out explicitly in his discussion of black children in South Central Harlem that their language is different, not inferior. It is more or less appropriate to certain environments. A particular code of language, then, like a particular mode of thought, has advantages and disadvantages. Sometimes middle class language is precise, elaborated, and logical; other times, though, it is redundant, passive, verbose, turgid, and empty.

There is no guarantee that Andy can learn academic reasoning at home. In this country, we value ethnic individuality. We are a nation of immigrants; even "native" Americans were immigrants thousands of years ago. According to demographic studies, there are an increasing number of socioeconomic and ethnic differences among our citizens. Even if people learn to speak the same language, however, they retain different patterns of behavior. Even more important, these cultures may understand the world differently. Some cultures, for example, stand close to one another when they talk; others keep a distance between them. Some groups gesture a lot; others, less. When we do international business, we consider their different understanding. Astute U. S. sales people are not offended, for example, if their Latino counterparts are late for appointments; they accept that Latin American cultures allocate time differently; if a superior has kept them, they expect an equal to understand. We recognize that it might shame Japanese workers to single them out for individual creativity, whereas it could be a valued reward to a worker in the United States. In the Middle East, business is often conducted slowly with the entire family or business group present; U. S. business people expect to have to take time to let their Arabian counterparts know and accept them. If there are basic cultural differences in how people understand time, success, and relationships, there are certainly different attitudes toward knowledge and learning. Even if students are not specifically identified with one ethnic group, their family group attitudes can promote or inhibit academic thinking in school. Andy learned his lessons well; he came to school with assumptions about learning and thinking. When he arrived at kindergarten with a commonsense mode of thinking rather than an academic mode, he found school learning difficult.

Clearly, the child learns feelings at home as well. In an electrical storm, my grandmother used to unplug all the electric appliances, pour out all standing water (and certainly never took a bath), and hide behind the downstairs living room couch. Whenever there was a storm, my mother would take me out on our side porch, point out the lightning, and say, "LOOK, isn't it beautiful?"; she wanted to teach me not to be so terrified as she had been taught to be by her mother. Explicitly, she did what all parents do implicitly, mostly by good or bad example—teach feelings: pleasure at a grandparent's visit, annoyance at a door-to-door salesman, excitement at a trip to the beach, boredom with the grocery store, love of your children, hatred toward assassins, acceptance of drug use or prejudice. Those feelings are connected to school as well as to family, friends, sex, food, clothing, housing, and work.

Children also learn feelings toward themselves, both at home and at school. Many of our students come from an unhappy early six years, plagued by personal difficulties like poverty, neglect, or abuse. Their later experiences, including school, family, and friends, can also foster feelings of self-hatred, rage, insecurity, fear, and power-lessness. These feelings inhibit their learning. By the time Andy arrived in my class, after years of failure in school, he felt worthless and hopeless.

We are victims of our own preconceptions. We call Andy stupid because of the way we define smart. Our goal should not be to label Andy. Nor should it be to eliminate his common sense (or his musical reasoning). It should be to give him an opportunity to reason academically when he chooses and the ability to decide when it is appropriate to choose academic thinking.

We owe Andy. We make him go to school. Then we make him feel stupid. He tries to please us with cookies and Christmas trees; we unconsciously judge his morality against Kohlberg's "universal principles" or "social contract" stages (1981) when Andy doesn't operate within those moral standards. When his active mind continues to work even though it can't grasp the classroom topic, we punish his "disruptive behavior." When he gives up, we criticize his "laziness." We grade him—at seventeen—against his ability to function on a high level of the academic continuum even though that pattern of thinking is unknown to him and uncharacteristic of most people most of the time.

Even more important though, as a *nation* we promised. We guaranteed Andy an equal opportunity to learn; but it is not equal to run a thoroughbred in the Indianapolis 500. Andy cannot be something he isn't. Equal job opportunities are often based on success in school: Andy can't be a doctor if he can't learn science. Besides, we also promised an equal opportunity for liberty and justice; education is supposed to help free him from the limitations of his birth as well as his own personal and social nearsightedness. While we do not expect every citizen to be a philosopher, we do expect every citizen to be able to vote freely and wisely. In fact, in twenty years I'll be counting on his vote to keep me out of nuclear war, protect my social security, and make sure there are ramps at the market for my wheelchair.

When school starts, there's still no guarantee that Andy will learn academic reasoning if he hasn't begun already at home. There is, of course, great interest in teaching thinking these days and considerable evidence that "critical" thinking can be taught (Dansereau et al. 1979; Lochhead and Clement 1979). However, what we're doing now in schools doesn't work. Many good teachers model the intellectual skills, not only of educated persons but also of their specific disciplines; some explicitly teach critical thinking based on the taxonomies of Ennis (1975), Feuerstein (1980), Guilford (1967) or Bloom (1956). There are also many programs disseminated across the country: Instrumental Enrichment, CoRT, TACTICS for Thinking, Philosophy for Children, Talents Unlimited, Project IMPACT, McRAT, HOTS, 4MAT, Learning to Learn, Illinois Thinking Project, the IDEAL Problem Solver, and so on. While there is some evidence that children score better on thinking skills tests, there is no evidence that these programs produce adults (or even seventeen-year-olds) who reason academically. Furthermore, these programs are available to proportionally few people and are difficult to integrate into a state-mandated curriculum.

Other teachers teach general "heuristics" to improve thinking. Unfortunately children cannot use a problem-solving approach like

Analyze the problem

Search for related knowledge

Plan possible solutions

Keep track of progress

Check the results against the plan

unless they can "analyze the problem." Problem-solving heuristics like this one do not address the particular skills that constitute every stage, even though these strategies may inadvertently exercise some of these skills as they go along. Andy would gladly learn the five stages of the process, but in a group problem-solving activity, he would be unable to analyze the problem and if he did, he would never be able to transfer this method to any other problem, the problem of being unable to study for tests, for example. These heuristics are useful only if there is enough class time—perhaps for Andy an entire semester—really to practice all the subskills of the method. They are no more useful to him, taught quickly, than teaching him to memorize the words "generalization," "illogical," and "non sequitur," and then expecting him to avoid general, illogical, and disorderly writing. Words do not improve children's thinking or writing if they cannot apply them.

Implicitly, we teach some composite skills—problem solving in algebra; generating, classifying, and ordering information in English; recalling information in social studies; and scanning and holding information in most reading and notetaking activities. When they are taught implicity, the teacher assumes the students can perform the mental and physical structuring necessary. To take notes, for example, a student must be able to listen, predict, sort out main ideas, order the ideas, visualize on the page, remember what to fill in later, fill in when there's a spare moment, and write simultaneously.

There's a high probability that if Andy is unsuccessful in first grade, he will be relatively more unsuccessful in twelfth. We cannot assume that academic reasoning develops naturally from common-sense reasoning anymore than we can assume that academic reasoning is the only "good" form of reasoning or that our "Western" developmental sequence is the only one. Academic reasoning is dependent on academic attitudes (motivation), which are learned at home before a child is five. It's also not taught to Andy in school. According to Goodlad (1984) and many others, "critical" thinking is taught and modeled in high-track classes; academic attitudes are also modeled in these classes. Low-track classes emphasize memorization of isolated facts and passive obedience; the students who need the most practice get the fewest opportunities. Another explanation, almost too simple to mention in these days of elegant theories, is that the better you think the faster you learn.

The only guarantee is: if Andy doesn't learn to reason academically at home or in school, he will fail many classes; he will feel inadequate, frustrated, and angry; he'll create havoc for his teachers; and he'll be disenfranchised as an American citizen. So we owe Andy; and if neuroscience and psychology don't provide a certain answer, we still have to teach him the skills, knowledge, and attitudes that he needs in school. We have to act, finally, on experience, concern, commitment, speculation, and faith.

Attitudes come first. For some students, difficulties are simply based on limited information and skills. A seventeen-year-old who gets most of his information from tabloids may have difficulty with an economics course. However, if the teacher provides enough experience and structure, he can learn. Project Headstart is based on the idea that more experiences increase the child's conceptual base and help him to learn; problem-solving writing approaches like Linda Flower's (1979) are based on the idea that practice with mental activities will improve learning. But not for Andy! He doesn't just have limited information. He also has a different set of attitudes, a different world view. It is useless to give him lectures or reading on Japanese economy, even if you teach your best. Start with something he knows—Mitsubishi, for example. Make a comparison, draw diagrams, and put up a chart. Go to the Japanese embassy to get full-color posters of Japanese products and bring in a retired Japanese businessman as guest speaker. Be visual, auditory, and tactile. Be "abstract sequential" and "random concrete" (Gregorc 1979). You will still end up with answers copied from the encyclopedia and an understanding that stops with "They make Sony."

"Do you *understand,* Andy?" simply means something different to Andy than to me! Before developing content concepts and skills, he needs to understand understanding. For Andy, "understand" in that sentence means "Andy, did you hear everything I said?" That, of course, is not the question I'm asking. I mean, "Did you reconstruct it so that it made sense to you, so you could explain it clearly to someone else, so you will remember it next Friday on the quiz, and so you will be able to apply it not only to the next unit but to your adult life?"

It isn't that he *won't* or even that he *can't* understand. He just *doesn't.* Common sense and academic reasoning conform to different sets of rules. Were you good at grammar in high school? I was. When Mrs. Raithel taught me grammar in Jefferson City (Missouri) Senior High School, she did it by rules. "A pronoun takes the place of a noun." I always identified pronouns correctly, but my friend Ralph? Almost never! Personal pronouns weren't so bad, but relative pronouns, interrogative pronouns, impersonal pronouns, and indefinite pronouns were impossible. "Just learn the rules!" I'd say. I'm fairly sure that Mrs. Raithel suspected, as I did, that Ralph was a mite stupid.

I now know, of course, that I never just learned by rules that "it" in "it is raining" was a pronoun because it took the place of a noun. I recognized "it" as a pronoun from all the semantic and structural clues I had from years of consciousness of language and language structure in an academic household. For instance, I can see myself when I wasn't even four years old, standing by the big, old, black telephone in my front hallway. I can hear my mom and dad telling me over and over that if I picked up the phone and someone asked for me, I must answer "This is Joan." I had to respond that way because "It's me" was wrong and "It's I" was awkward. Such explicit, concious, abstract rules about language were foreign to Ralph.

He'd had years of experience with language also—beautiful, metaphorical, allusive, vivid, but centrally different from mine. My twelfth birthday is a good example. I had a roller skating party, and

I ignored my friend Ralph all afternoon. I guess being the center of attention made me a little uppity. Ralph had carefully saved his money to buy me a rhinestone necklace at Woolworths. Halfway through the party, he shoved the gift at me and said, "you'll just throw it away anyway." Later, we sat outside the skating rink and talked about friendship, social class, and, particularly, uppitiness. He managed that difficult conversation with subtlety and delicacy. But if I tried to quote him now, his words wouldn't seem beautiful or even sensible. When we sat there outside Roll-A-Round Rink, Ralph's face was alive and his body alert every minute. He told poignant stories about his feelings; he made ironic references to his poverty. He raised his hands, and touched my arm, and smiled appealingly, all at the right moments of his speech. His inflections mattered; his silences were dramatic.

However, Ralph's speech then, like all his conversation, was dependent on social intimacy. His family was crowded into three rooms; his neighborhood was poor and isolated from the rest of our town. Mostly, he spent his time with the same people, his six brothers and sisters and his many cousins, on Jackson Street in front of his house, All his life, he'd talked to an audience with shared assumptions, experiences, values, and goals. When they didn't understand him, they let him know on the spot. The context determined his lexical and syntactic choices. He had always cared about how he *uttered* words, not how he put them together. Their richness and harmony grew from that context.

He wasn't constrained, or enriched, by the same rules of "educated" language that I was. He couldn't really even conceive of language as separate from himself. Neither he nor his culture needed and valued my kind of logic, classification, or explicit rules. So no amount of repetition of the definition of pronouns would help Ralph identify pronouns to Mrs. Raithel's satisfaction, even though he knew perfectly well how to use them. Neither Ralph nor I knew then what I had that he didn't. We both thought I was just smarter. I wasn't.

Andy cannot choose to think as I do anymore than Ralph could choose to understand language as I did. While Andy enjoyed the irony of the "hot" or rather "lukewarm" Christmas tree, the further implications—moral or intellectual; social, political, or religious— were not especially relevant for him.

Academic morality, like academic intelligence, is defined by a hidden set of assumptions. For the most part, these assumptions are parallel to our assumptions in schools about intellectual maturity. Whatever we do in our personal lives, we talk as though we accept Kohlberg's hierarchy of moral development, and we judge people immoral when they don't reason like Socrates. When I was on a field trip with Andy once, we were in an elevator with eight other students. On the 59th floor, five boys started jumping up and down. And Maria, one of the girls, started crying; Andy put his arms around her and held her all the way to the first floor, despite the contempt he was likely to get from his classmates. I told him, "Andy, I appreciate the way you took care of Maria; she was really scared." He said, "I know."

Andy isn't immoral. His commonsense morality doesn't value either introspection or analysis of other's feelings. In fact, he regards psychology and psychiatry as dangerous. He cannot alone change himself because he cannot objectively, scientifically, stand back and collect data about his own feelings, motives, faults, and virtues. He cannot make hypotheses about his behavior or flexibly revise his actions or attitudes. Similarly, he cannot "walk around in my shoes" because he doesn't imagine that anyone feels any different than he does. He tries to please me by what would please him. He doesn't know that the people who owned the tree might have treasured it. He doesn't know that my reputation might be hurt if I have a stolen Christmas tree in my classroom. He doesn't know that "Can I get away with it?" is not the main question to ask or even a significant one. He doesn't want to know that half-off the property is also half-on. He doesn't know that that society is held together by a "social contract" and that people must voluntarily protect the entire system not just their friends and favorite teachers.

Of course, Andy has been *told* social/moral rules: "Don't steal." "Don't lie." Ralph was told rules for grammar and usage, but he couldn't apply those academic rules in his writing and speech because he hadn't internalized them in his early years. Andy has the same trouble with academic moral rules. They don't seem automatic or sensible to him. In the "educated" world, stealing is wrong; but you can cheat on your income taxes; you can also get a break on the cost of carrots if the checker rings it wrong or a low price on a leather coat if it's marked wrong in the store. You shouldn't bend the rules about Christmas trees half on the road, but it's just fine to have an illegal apartment in your house. The rules of morality that really make sense are the ones you internalized when you were young. Common sense can include a different mode of morality just as Ralph's "street language" was a different code of communication and expression. More than codes of language, however, modes of morality and school learning impose on others; stealing a Christmas tree imposes not only on the victim, but on me, the recipient of a "hot" item. In my world, Andy's particular "situational ethics" are unacceptable. Andy's behavior was wrong, but he is not culpable. The school system is guilty.

   Schools *do* make a difference. What you don't learn before five, you learn after five; and the place you learn most outside of home is school. We don't want to improve Andy's commonsense thinking; we want to teach him **how** to think in another pattern. Unless we can teach Andy academic attitudes and show him their value both in some content areas of school and in some aspects of everyday life, Andy—and his teachers—will continue to suspect he is just a mite stupid *and* more than a mite bad.

Chapter Three

The Secret Code
Average Students at Risk

Intellectual freedom is essential to human society . . . Freedom of thought is the only guarantee against an infection of people by mass myths which, in the hands of treacherous demagogues, can be transformed into bloody dictatorships.
Andrei Sakharov

My custodian is delighted that he can name the capitals of all the states. One day, as I came into the high school, he hurried up and said, "I've asked everyone who's come into the building this morning and all the secretaries in the front office. I'll bet you can't name seven kinds of pronouns!"

He's bought it. Don's bought the whole educational system without wondering why a person wants to know seven kinds of pronoun. "So what?" would have been rude. So would "What do the seven kinds of pronouns really mean in your life, Don?" "So what?" is too late, anyway. It's the question the system never asked him!

If you'd asked when he was seventeen, "What is education for?" he might have said "to learn." If you'd pressed him, "To learn for what purpose?" he might have said "To get a better job" or "To get into college." He probably gives those reasons to his own children now. But he wouldn't understand if you asked him, "How did school change you, Don?"

Our Constitution assumes that humanity's role is to progress toward a better life. People do not simply adjust to a fixed physical and social reality, but recreate their world by seeing it as a series of questions to answer, challenges to overcome, problems to solve, tasks to accomplish, and goals to achieve. Unlike other animals, we are aware of ourselves as separate from the spatial and temporal world. We *can* change; we can set goals, evaluate ourselves, and revise our behavior. We are educated, not trained. The world is the milieu in which we produce objects, institutions, ideas, and dreams.

Education develops people's intellectual power to overcome obstacles to freedom, equality, and justice. Even though we are born with limits, we can become more free. Even though we are born unequal, we can, and should, create equal opportunities. Our ancestors, our neighbors, our scientists, our historians, and our poets have created our world view. As a culture, we forged our ideas; we can restructure them. Slaves are only slaves in a culture that has created slavery. What caused the Quakers in the eighteenth century to revile slavery? Could the abolitionists understand the feelings of the slaves? Other economic systems? A different meaning of the human spirit? What educational experiences did they have? And Gandhi? How could he have learned so much from Thoreau who was an ocean, a culture, and fifty years away? How did he know that his people could be free?

Learning all the state capitals does not have the goal of learning all the state capitals—although Don probably thinks it does. He thinks, if he thinks about it at all, that the main goal of learning is remembering. He also seems to think that the main reward for remembering is approval from his teachers, even now when he and I are adults. He doesn't know that knowledge and skills are also tools which he needs to be a happier, more powerful person. Maybe he can be happy without them, maybe he will not. Those tools don't guarantee him happiness and effectiveness, but they give him one more opportunity for understanding and changing his own life.

Unfortunately he, and others like him, can grow up to be victims. They can be tyrannized not only by external forces like politics and advertising, but also by their own attitudes and feelings. We all know someone who is terrified of dogs; it generally doesn't help to say, "Hey, it's just a little dog." Many people cannot analyze the situation, consider that the creature is eighteen inches long, realize that their fear is probably unrelated to this animal, and act on the assumption that if other people are not afraid, they should not be. Their fear of dogs overrides logic; and they are incapacitated by that fear. A fear of dogs is much easier to overcome than fear of failure, public humiliation, or abandonment. I have students who won't go into certain classes because people stare at them, won't phone for information because they don't know what to say, and won't write legibly because they can't spell. They are tyrannized because they do not have tools to understand and direct those feelings.

Their security depends on fortuitous external circumstances—a happy marriage, a good job, clear weather, or a benevolent government. They are tyrannized by bad luck or bad planning. The science teacher down the hall from me has a student who panics every time he loses his car keys (about twice a month); he rushes off to hunt for them during a chemistry exam, a lecture, or a lab. George, the student, really can't consider other ways of dealing with the fear or, in fact, his carelessness. He will probably vote impulsively too. Many people do; they vote on appealing personalities or controversial single issues. Tommy Mack, whose brother is a state trooper, voted for a law-and-order candidate in the last state election. He was legitimately concerned about crime in his neighborhood. Now, he is outraged when the local police stop his son to search his trunk for drugs and, in the process, break all the expensive cosmetic samples which his daughter carries there to sell. He sees no connection. He doesn't habitually see the whole system or recognize his part in it. For many Americans happiness and fulfillment also depend on externals. Tommy's life is boring without the horror film, the new relationship, the highway accident, or the scandal sheet.

If health, wealth, excitement, and love don't happen along, Don and George do not know how to create them. Moreover, and more important, they do not know they *can* create them. Why? Because we don't teach them.

People come to school with a variety of preconceptions: some are called "beliefs"; some "attitudes"; some "feelings"; some "habits"; some "knowledge." They include ideas about religion, manners, reality, beauty, and justice. The preconceptions related to attitudes, feelings and habits are often called "gut feelings" or "intuition." The ones related to knowledge, religion, and reality are often called "truth."

Attitudes, feelings, and habits come from experience. Our personal experiences determine many of our personal attitudes about ourselves and our relation to society: feelings of self-esteem, power, competence, acceptance, and lovableness. Abused children often feel unattractive and sexually-abused children often think they must be passive and agreeable in order to be loved, however attractive and lovable they are from other people's perspectives. Not that they could articulate those preconceptions; they simply perceive and act on them.

Feelings are determined by preconceptions: happiness, sadness, fear, guilt. I am predisposed to think that I'm a basically O.K., smart-enough person, and that most people will, at worst, be indifferent to me. If I don't quite know what to say on the phone, it doesn't matter.

I know that my English skills are good enough that a spelling mistake here or there is immaterial. Many students, however, don't have preconceptions of their own competence and acceptability. Their preconceptions about themselves are debilitating in academic and social situations. Andy, the student who brought me the Christmas tree, certainly came to school with feelings and attitudes that were antithetical to learning; he had a poor self-image and great diffidence.

Students also come to school with attitudes and habits acquired from their culture, family, and peers. Everyone has them: "language is a valuable way to learn" or "language is a dangerous trap to avoid"; "history is essental" or "useless"; "school success deprives a boy of his manliness" or "school success enhances a boy's manliness," "girls are bad in math," "boys don't like to read." The entire, combined set of attitudes and values make up a subculture's "world view," that is the culture's combined preconceptions about truth, reality, learning, and meaning. All of those attitudes, and many others, influence a child's learning.

Many children come to school valuing education: they want to "do well"; their parents, like Don, want them to "do good in school." However, children in our schools come from many ethnic, religious, ideological, and economic backgrounds. So, mixed in with those positive intentions, are a variety of assumptions about the goals of school, the nature of learning, the role of language, and the characteristics of adulthood. In certain subcultures, it's rude to question and analyze, for example; in others it's a mark of intelligence. Cultures and individuals disagree substantially, though not always explicitly, about the role of individual citizens in relation to the community, one of the central issues in democracy. Robert Coles (1990) finds five quite different attitudes among our children on that one issue: he claims that twenty-five percent of our children are civic humanists (do what is best for the community), twenty percent conventionalists (defer to authority), eighteen percent expressivists (do whatever feels good), sixteen percent theists (do what is dictated by religion), and 10 percent utilitarians (do whatever gets what you want). Children's assumptions about the role of individuals in society are only one of the thousands of assumptions they bring to school.

We don't tell students explicitly that we make "academic" assumptions about knowing, learning, communicating, and behaving. When teachers talk to one another, we say we value perceiving, labeling, classifying, organizing, and remembering as tools. We claim to value detachment from our immediate circumstances and our cultural and environmental world view. In goal statements, we list self-critical analysis and free choice. In classes, we expect students to plan, to set goals, to persist, to revise, to remain flexible, to reevaluate. In our English classes, we say we encourage multiple meanings and symbolism; and in science we say we teach them to use language which is accurate, logical, and context-free. Theoretically, we want students to be able to choose their language and mode of expression the way they should be able to choose their lifestyles, their beliefs, and their consequences. Yet do we ever share these assumptions with students? No, we never mention the purpose of "academic thinking." We don't tell them that we assume academic thinking gives them power and freedom. We don't say clearly that we're helping them organize perception and conception differently or that we want them to be able to take more informed, skilled actions.

Our structure doesn't imply that message any better than our words teach it explicitly. Everything we actually do in school (our curriculum, methods, and organization) suggests the opposite, that we value storing data. Our teachers are, in general, "authorities" and our students are passive recipients of our ideas. We lecture and we assign reading. We choose the literature in English and hand out the current events in social studies. In some states ninth-and tenth-grade global studies courses cram information about the entire world into two years. When you look at state curriculum outlines, you see that children in tenth grade are supposed to remember more pieces of information than most adults already know. We claim we teach academic thinking, but we deny our claims by most of our choices.

Most skills, except for reading and writing, are taught accidentally, as by-products. Social studies teachers often say, "of course I teach thinking while I'm giving them the information." All students do, however, is identify and remember. The teacher and the textbook do all the work; students listen to lectures and read the packaged material. If, occasionally, they classify, hypothesize, and conclude, it's not on new material. There's very little uncertainty and very little opportunity to make decisions, complete projects, or develop meaning.

School is unreal. In most classrooms, there are no compelling reasons to solve problems. In mathematics, students have all the information they need; they are doing exercises in a closed system. History and science have most of the answers in the textbooks, data sheets, and blackboards. Children think that scientific research involves reproducing Mendel's experiences and that historical research is going to the library and copying information onto three-by-five cards with the main idea in the upper left hand corner. Similarly, most high school students think that the point of literature is to remember the plot and find the metaphors. After all aren't most of the test questions about plot and most of the discussion about metaphors? They think the purpose of school reading is reading. Students are only expected to deal with the information given, whether it is the past, the environment, or a novel. Classes are repetitions of others' thoughts and research. We don't teach the academic thinking that Don and Andy need.

No wonder more than half of our children cheat on tests. Why not? If it's simply a matter of a few pieces of information they've missed, what difference does it make to them if they cheat once or twice? They have no idea that the point isn't a few facts. Actually, most students are satisfied with the "ground-to-be-covered" method; it's safe and predictable. They put in their time and pass their tests; they get *C*'s and *B*'s and they think that they are successful.

In the real world, they are not successful; information isn't packaged so neatly. We teach citizenship: students learn the three branches of government, the election process, and the "unwritten Constitution," but proportionally few vote or fill in their census forms. They sit in global studies for two years and memorize the map of the Soviet Union, the history of the Cold War, and the concept of nationalism, but how many paid any attention to the cataclysmic changes in the Soviet Union in 1989–1992? Why vote? Why read the national news? They approach citizenship with boredom and a "what-can-I-do-about-it?" attitude.

They don't know that "the only freedom that is of enduring importance is the freedom of intelligence, that is to say, freedom of observation and of judgment exercised in behalf of purposes that are intrinsically worthwhile" (Dewey 1938). They don't recognize that it is their job to reconstruct their society. Our practice teaches them otherwise. They don't know that education is the basis of democracy; that in school they are supposed to be learning to think so they can continue to create a system that is better and better. They keep on memorizing.

There's a secet code in our schools, a secret pattern of thought, and we set up a system where students can't break it because they don't even know it's there. We tell Don in every way that the purpose of school is remembering. He believes it and is proud of his seven kinds of pronouns.

There are children who learn the code. They learn our well-kept secret at home. In those homes, "academic" education is practiced. People sit down to meals together and discuss the news. What's happening in the Soviet Union and how is it related to the Cold War? The words *perestroika* and *glasnot* are used. At night, there are bedtime stories. Sometimes when the parents read stories such as Sendak's Wild Things, they discuss the pictures. "Why do you think the wild things look like that?" they ask. "Do you have wild things in yourself?" When their parents watch television or read, the family talks about the programs and the books. They question and argue and discuss. They choose words carefully and use them accurately. Ideas are important. They go to the library; they have magazines in the house. So do their friends and their friends' children. The children hear and see and do and practice the household attitudes, skills, and knowledge from birth. They are no more conscious of their goals and attitudes than Don is; but unlike Don they come to school already equipped with "academic" patterns of mind.

The ones who learn the code at home succeed on memory tests because memory is best when it is actively incorporated into meaningful patterns; but they know more. They question; they connect; they hypothesize. Even before they enter school, they know they can change the world through intellect. They are more than equal because others have no choice but inequality. They will have more power over their health, because they have power over their environment. They will contribute more to their society because they will learn more. They will receive more justice because they will demand and create it.

In other homes, education is valued, but this kind of "academic" education is not practiced. Children learn different lessons about what is important, how to act, how to respond to newspapers and books, and how to spend leisure time. When they get to school, they do not have the experience in academic skills, attitudes, or knowledge. Trying as hard as they can, they are still memorizing facts without years of background, years of practice learning and patterning. They think they just aren't smart, and they settle for what states like to call "competence." Their inability to match the performance of other students who have an advantage makes them feel powerless in school and in society; or maybe they succeed on those tests and they think they are educated, but ultimately they do not have the intellectual equipment to control and enrich their lives.

Many of these children, like Don, get along; in school he was responsible and obedient. Unlike Andy, he "made it." He has a job, a wife, a home. He was never "at risk" in the same way. I asked Don once, "What kind of student were you, Don?" He said, "Average." I expect he was. Average can mean anything. It could mean that he had access to a variety of thinking patterns—commonsense, academic, symbolic, musical, and spatial—and he chose freely to disregard grades. "Average" could also mean he had so many problems that school was not his first priority. However, it usually means that he did not have access to those thinking patterns we rely on covertly, and, in fact, he did not know that they existed. He was given a recipe for a cake which will always be a little flat, a little hard, a little tasteless. There are secret ingredients he no longer has access to. He is not poisoned, but he is not well-nourished either.

The Great Roe is one of Woody Allen's creatures: "The Great Roe is a mythologial beast with the head of a lion and the body of a lion, though not the same lion" (1975). My custodian, Don is definitely not mythological. He's a real person in the present time. Like most real people, Don entered school Don and exited school Don and it was the *same* Don.

Most children do not come out of school substantially different from the way they went in, at least in terms of thinking patterns. This situation is not justice and equality; it means that people do not have equal access to jobs. A person who can't think in certain ways cannot be a psychiatrist, a teacher, a physicist, a corporation executive, or a lawyer. It means that many people do not have equal access to happiness and power. Fewer than twenty-five percent of our students really excel in school. Don was average; Don made *B*'s and *C*'s. Unfortunately, we don't live in Lake Wobegon where "the children are all above average." Fifty percent of our children are average.

Formal education should involve rebirth. A piano teacher does not claim to help restructure a person's mind. She teaches a skill; people go to the piano teacher because they want piano playing. But young people go to a history teacher for reasons they don't understand and often can't discover. "History doing" is bigger than a skill; history (and physics and literature) is another code for understanding the world.

Teaching is an ethical act. The purpose of high school, the purpose of teaching, is to help children change, to help children answer the questions "What is my life?" and "How shall I live it?" It is not to help them get a *B* or get a diploma or even to remember state capitals. True education is the opportunity for intellectual freedom.

Chapter Four

The Pattern That Connects
What Is Thinking?

My sometime-student Dave spends most of his time on the streets. He's clever and curious about life and the people around him. He knows how different families live in his impoverished neighborhood, speculates on their motivations, and predicts their behavior fairly accurately. However, he neither reads nor does he attend school often. He finds the far future and the distant past inconceivable, and he has little framework for understanding the Cargo Cult or the federal government.

Dave's upstairs neighbor, Anna, is the youngest of nine children in an extremely chaotic household. Maybe that's part of the reason she spends hours in the public library. She knows about the Cargo Cult, King Lear and the impact three administrations had on the war in Vietnam much better than she knows Dave's family.

Both Dave and Anna are in my eleventh-grade U. S. history and government class. By eleventh grade a person may be familiar primarily with his or her own neighborhood or may have vicariously experienced many worlds in the present, past, future, and fantasy. Students also come to my class with different attitudes toward learning. Dave thinks school is a waste. Who needs it? He can make more money working in a carpet clearance warehouse and much more money hustling full-time. Learning is to keep out of trouble, make money, and help your friends. Anna's whole life is in books. Learning is new worlds to see, new ways to understand; it is friendship and family. And everything she reads fits into her preconceptions and builds new ideas. They also have quite different skills. Anna's language skills are prodigious. She reads and writes effec-

tively and delights in Latin and Greek roots. She outlines her extremely orderly and cynical papers, and her humor is all word play.
Dave's language is allusive, metaphoric, and colorful but almost
entirely oral, full of stories, gestures and movement. Dave isn't stupid. Although he sometimes reasons "logically," academic and symbolic thinking simply aren't comfortable patterns of mind for him.

They are, unfortunately for Dave, the patterns required in U. S.
history and government. If Dave is going to learn U. S. history, if,
indeed, he is going to complete high school successfully, he has to
master those patterns of mind. How did Dave and Anna develop so
differently when they grew up in the same apartment building? They
went to the same elementary, middle and high schools. They even
"party" with the same friends! In order to teach Dave and Anna, we
need to know what thinking is, how Dave and Anna think, and what
experiences we can provide them in the classroom to change their
thinking.

"Thought" is certainly "real"; the word describes a "real" force,
like gravity. We can perceive the effects; we can guess at the environmental and biological factors which influence those effects. However,
words such as "thinking," "concepts," and "memory" have no material referents. Bloom (1956), Guilford (1957), Feuerstein (1980), and
Sternberg (1988) all provide useful descriptions of possible cognitive
processes, but there is no correct taxonomy of thought. The best we
can do, as teachers, is to pool our own observations of our students'
thinking and learning and to develop our own definitions. Our definitions need to be simple because our goal is to use them quickly and
flexibly in class to help Dave, as well as Andy, Don and Anna.

We know what thinking isn't. It isn't just movies of the world
filmed by a sensory camera and projected onto Dave's mind. Between
the time he perceives and conceives, Dave's mind acts on the world;
it orders, classifies, transforms, stores, recalls, and represents what it
sees, feels, hears, smells, and tastes. Somehow, it acts through the
nervous system. The particular concepts formed then influence subsequent perception.

Conceptions and perceptions flow through his mind constantly.
There are always interactions between this internal stream and the
external world. There are also interactions with other people's con-
structions and perceptions. Reading and writing, selling a rug, and
playing softball engage Dave's inner stream actively. Walking down
the road or sitting in class often allow the inner stream to flow more
freely. Dave is thinking constantly.

Lucy Sprague Mitchell (1971) describes two stages of learning: 1)
acquiring concepts by perception; and 2) relating them to other
external phenomena and also to concepts already in the mind. These

two parts of thinking are inseparable. There is no perception without preconception. If observation occurred without preconceptions, the world would flash by and not register at all—William James' "great blooming, buzzing, confusion." Mental actions connect preconceptions to the external world; without them there would be only unsorted sights, sounds, smells, tastes, and feels. Similarly, mental actions allow us to reconceive what's already in our minds; without mental actions we would have no ideas.

I can provisionally describe all this structuring and connecting simply in five basic mental actions: 1) discriminating parts; 2) finding likenesses; 3) finding differences; 4) grouping; and 5) ordering. Those five are arbitrary, of course. I might have said that the first three were basic because "grouping" is really "finding a central likeness." Or I could have added one more: 6) transferring principles of grouping. However, transferring principles (such as seeing the homologous relationship between horses' hooves and human fingernails) is really just finding likenesses which are more removed from sensory existence.

Dave is in high school now, but these same five mental actions occurred when he was a baby. Eye scan studies show that even infants move their eyes from part to part of a dog just as they move their fingers over a rattle. So when toddlers first point and say "doggie," they already have concepts of proportion, number, size, shape, hardness, texture, sound, and movement. Slightly older children can quickly discriminate parts, identify likenesses and differences, extract main characteristics and group those characteristics well enough to tell a dog from a cat. Most dogs have tails. While they have many types of tails (curly, straight, stubby, sticking up, and flopping down), they never have cat tails. Even if they have no tails at all, very young children know enough abstracted qualities of dogs that they can easily distinguish tailless dogs from baboons.

By adolescence, most of us understand much more abstract and more general concepts than "dog," but the basic mental actions are the same. Throughout childhood and early adolescence, for example, you probably had recurrent, unnoticed experiences with the concept of "spottiness." You experienced polka-dotted dresses, dirty spots on the floor, chicken pox, a dalmatian named "Spot," and a commercial on television about "drops that spot," as well as metaphors like a "spotty career." Slowly, and probably unconsciously, you separated the parts and stripped away the irrelevant details of color, texture, smell, purpose, and result. Then you found the traits common to spottiness and rejected the superfluous ones. You abstracted, composed, and organized those traits. Now you know "spottiness!" You can not only recognize unfamiliar types of spots, but also understand imaginary, metaphorical spots as in "a cold lemonade hits the spot." As an adult, you go through the same process when you repeatedly encounter words such as "concept" and "metacognition" in books about teaching thinking. Slowly, the concept emerges, through those same five basic mental actions.

Anna is extremely creative and intuitive; even her unique imagination involves these same five mental actions. She simply groups unexpected elements. Once, when we were doing a project teaching vocabulary to young children, Anna decided to create a "morpho-meaning" coloring book. She illustrated the meanings of phrases like "nuclear fusion" with humorous cartoons, based on visual puns. She put thirty "morpho-meanings" on 18" x 36" paper, bound them, made copies, and distributed the coloring books to children in the first and second grades. She had made a connection among word play, picture play, and hand play that's unique in teaching advanced vocabulary to young children. It worked. Many of her teachers just marvel at what they call her "divergent thinking" and "inspiration." She finds likenesses no one else even perceives, but she still is just discriminating parts, seeing likenesses and differences, grouping, and ordering.

Those five mental actions are simple. They are common to all people. They are the way all concepts develop. What is difficult, what distinguishes Anna from Dave, and what we have to consider more carefully is the particular concepts that these mental actions form and connect.

If you ask most people, "what is a concept?" they say "words" or "pictures" "in their heads." Some psychologists say that all concepts are verbal; others claim that language is not the fundamental symbolic system and that concepts are stored in words, figures, visual pictures, aural or motor sequences, and diagrams. Psychologists speculate that the brain builds mental models to organize and store reality: network models, prototype models, space models, or dictionary models. All these models from cognitive psychology and information processing, though, are just metaphors, no more scientifically accurate than the metaphors of Aristotle and Locke. They don't describe anything that physically exists anywhere. We don't know what concepts are.

I like to imagine adolescents' concepts as shining disco balls flashing in a dimly lit roller rink, rays of light reflecting different colors and intensities, intersecting the rays from other glittering balls and mingling with the rolling wheels and sweaty, swirling bodies. *That* model is still far too simple. No one can construct a model of the simplest concept. Even for those concepts that have names, the word is an abstraction of the concept. The word can be defined, but the concept can't. A concept is both bigger and smaller than the sum of its parts. It is bigger because it includes associations, implications, and ambiguities. It has unclear boundaries and similar ideas get confused. But it is smaller because it is an abstraction also. The concept "animal" loses all its details—wagging tail, doggy smell, soft fur, and barking sound. A concept is also impermanent; you forget parts. It is often unconscious. We do know that concepts even in young children are infinitely more complex than any schematic model.

My shining disco ball, as well as all other models, is also inadequate because concepts are dynamic. They are clusters of knowledge, attitudes, and skills, constantly interacting, restructuring, and responding. Seemingly simple ideas like "cat" may begin with sensory characteristics of sight, touch, taste, smell and sound, but even before she could say "ferret" my daughter Julia knew that Mikey, a friend's ferret, was definitely not a cat even though she'd never seen a ferret. She also knew that Mikey was somehow wonderful and strange. She knew that although cats had sharp claws, they are relatively safe. As she got older, she acquired more cultural and personal attitudes toward them. Virtually everyone in our culture accepts that cats, symbolically, are sneaky and sinister; they have nine lives. Literature, mythology, and history are full of cats. Besides, everyone has personal experiences with cats. For me, "cat" includes the joy of many Christmasses I spent with my Aunt Helen. When I was eight, she had a twenty-five-year-old cat named Tommy, who answered the telephone. Any normal person could, if she wanted, more than fill a book just with her knowledge and attitudes about cats. "Cat" is a relatively simple concept. Other concepts, like evil or Vietnam, could fill volumes from just one person's mind. In fact, they have (Russell, J. 1977). In order to teach, we have to know what cognitive volumes Anna and Dave bring to class with them.

What knowledge, attitudes, and skills do they bring that we have to build on? Simple knowledge itself isn't simple. Knowledge is recollections of places, times, people, objects, events, ideas, and patterns. Sometimes people distinguish between facts and concepts. But facts are always concepts and parts of concepts. The date 1776 is a concept itself and a significant part of many other concepts: "freedom," "democracy," and "revolution," for example.

There are different types of knowledge concepts. "Knowing" a cat is different from "knowing" a corporation is different from "knowing" gravity. A cat exists primarily in a sensory world, a corporation exists more in a world of relationships among people and systems, and gravity exists more as a hypothetical relationship among relationships. Dave knows many more concepts of physical objects than relationships among systems. He also knows ideas like "loyalty" and "honor." Other ideas, "existentialism," for example, hold no interest for him, and he doesn't wonder about ultimate meanings. Dave accepts his Baptist background without much question. Anna, on the other hand, wants to know about her relationship with the universe. She really considers her Catholic background; she thinks it's worthwhile to question the meaning of life.

However, it's not just that Anna knows more words or that Dave and Anna know different words. In class, Anna and Dave know many of the same words; but they know them differently. When we discuss "force," in U. S. history, Dave conceives physical force. Anna is familiar with systems and complex interrelations within systems. She understands world economy and considers the individual degradation that even economic sanctions impose on people.

Along with their knowledge concepts, Dave and Anna have different cultural and personal attitudes. "Facts," sensory characteristics of physical objects, and ideas are never held "in mind" isolated. Concepts about dogs or justice or science are always ethnocentric. Whether you think of dogs as food depends on where you live, whether you think of romantic love at all depends on when you lived. Anna's and Dave's knowledge depends on their world view, their own or their society's set of assumptions about reality, truth, and knowledge—their unconscious philosophy. Their behavior toward learning also depends on their social and personal attitudes. If Anna were a traditional Japanese child, in a traditional Japanese culture, for example, she might be humiliated by, rather than proud of, the reputation she has for unconventionality.

Dave and Anna also come to class with quite different skills and methods. Skills and methods are concepts about how to behave. Skills and methods can be entirely mental or mental and physical; they include social behavior, writing styles, and inquiry methods. Some of these strategies are everyday how-to's: how to cook or how to identify propaganda. Speaking, reading, and writing are skills; so are notetaking, freewriting, and meditation. School learning always involves acquiring skills and methods.

Many skills, some highly complex, are unconcious—speaking, for example. Children begin with hit-or-miss methods. My son Christopher, at nine months, played with a Tupperware toy that had yellow shapes to fit into a blue and red hollow dodecahedron with a hole for each shape. He would bang a yellow cylinder repeatedly on a square blue hole, then on a hexagonal hole, then on the trapezoidal one, and maybe, with luck, on the circle. At five or six, though, he looked at the yellow hexahedron and then found the hexagonal hole with his eyes. The method is conscious. Later, picking the right hole became almost automatic. Older children unconsciously ride a bicycle with perfect balance, turn the water faucet for the tub clockwise, and pick up the receiver on the ringing phone right side up.

Like Christopher, Dave and Anna have developed methods and skills that have become automatic. They are both skilled in communication, for example. Dave's skills are oral; Anna's are written. Dave is loud, charismatic, and funny—in the lunchroom. In the classroom, he seems disruptive and rude. Anna is satiric on paper; in classroom discussion, she seems withdrawn and perhaps sullen. Both rely on those skills and are inhibited by them.

Dave and Anna think differently; their knowledge, attitudes, and skills are different. They have different "patterns of mind." A "pattern of mind" is a particular combination of knowledge, attitudes, and skills that is distinguishable from other combinations; the pattern should help people acquire information and solve problems. Anna and Dave (and their teachers) come to class bound by their patterns of knowledge, attitudes and skills. In his senior year, Dave will be expected to read, understand, and remember a chapter in his economics text on capitalism in China. He is not supposed to think "Who cares?" "What use is this to a rug salesman?" "I don't want to learn about those communists! You can't persuade me to be a communist!" or any of the other comments which he has actually said to me about similar topics. Anna will be much more successful in senior economics. She is not, however, necessarily smarter nor does she think better. She thinks differently.

Good thinking is not just one particular set of knowledge, attitudes, and skills. Howard Gardner has outlined possibilities for "multiple intelligences" (1983). He infers seven different "intelligences" from research in psychology, sociology, and neuroscience: logico-mathematical, musical, spatial, linguistic, bodily-kinesthetic, interpersonal, and intrapersonal. From the point of view of teaching, I prefer to think in terms of five patterns that are more easily observable in schools. Of course, any definitions of patterns will be inexact. However, in order to teach Anna and Dave, it's useful to think about the way they solve problems and get information in terms of my five patterns: academic sense, common sense, symbolic sense, musical sense, and spatial sense.

The academic pattern of mind emphasizes understanding the external world and our relationship to it. Its ultimate purpose is considering and controlling external phenomena. Its skills are "scientific": collecting data, forming hypotheses or theories, testing these theories, and revising them when necessary. It is the pattern of mind described by Piaget (1954) and Bloom (1956). It is the dominant form of thinking expected in sciences and social studies; it is in large part the thinking pattern expected in literature studies and in advanced mathematics. The academic pattern also is employed in the approaches to understanding yourself and others described by Erikson (1964), Freud (1989), and Kohlberg (1972). This kind of self-knowledge and knowledge of others is based on scientific detachment and desire to change. Standing outside yourself or your associates and trying to identify, label, speculate about, and change your feelings is similar to studying DNA. Academic thinking is characteristic of modern Western cultures. It involves elaborate symbolic thinking and fine distinctions and classifications. Schools emphasize all aspects of academic thinking except personal analysis. It is the pattern which characterizes Anna.

Dave's characteristic pattern, common sense, also focuses on understanding the world and our relation to it with the purpose of controlling the external phenomena. However, common sense is more like faith than science. It accepts the values of its culture. Common sense focuses on the same general areas of life: history, science, some language and mathematics as well as self and others. However, its goal is immediate action rather than reflection. The speech tends to be what Basil Bernstein (1979) calls "restricted" rather than "elaborated" codes; language is also narrative rather than logical. Certainly people using common sense use hypotheses, but they do so quickly and with less data. Common sense is "intuitive," rapid, and practical. Common sense is inflexible and resistant to change. Reasoning is more to justify existing beliefs and actions than to disprove hypotheses.

The symbolic pattern of mind focuses on representation and systems of representation. I'm using the common meaning of the word *symbol,* "to represent something else," such as, a flag, a song, or a phrase. This definition includes the semiotician's "icons" and all other kinds of representation. Meaning comes from a culture or community. There are a variety of symbolic patterns that Americans need to learn: verbal languages, mathematics, musical notation, diagrams, maps, graphs, computer languages, movement patterns (in classical ballet, for example), and social gestures.

The attitude characteristic of symbolic thinking is attraction to abstraction and representation. Dave is accurate and competent in reading and writing, but he has no particular enthusiasm for language. Anna loves words and word play. One of her drawings still hangs on my classroom wall. She gave it to me when she graduated. It's a caricature huddled in the shadow under a long shelf. The title is "A shadow of her former shelf." Accomplished verbal thinking like this requires a love of ambiguity and multiplicity. It is Bernstein's "elaborated code." Accomplished mathematical thinking, however, which never appealed to Anna, requires a love of clarity and condensation of meaning. Characteristically, words are used to explore human complexity and mathematical symbols are used to manipulate abstractions devoid of the difficulties of human relationships.

Symbolic thinking and academic thinking are interdependent. Symbolic disciplines, such as advanced mathematics and verbal languages, are essential to academic disciplines. Science, for example, requires both advanced mathematics and academic language; history requires words, diagrams, maps and graphs. Academic disciplines, such as history, are necessary to symbolic disciplines like writing. Writing is not just encoding and decoding; to write and read well (in Western terms), students must have the kind of knowledge, attitudes and "logical" reasoning characteristic of social studies. Similarly, advanced mathematics requires the logical skills of science as well as encoding abilities.

Musical and spatial patterns focus on the sensory parts of the world. Music looks at sound—rhythm, loudness, timbre, sound patterns. Spatial thinking focuses on form, movement, distance, color, light, proportion, relationship, perspective, texture, order and visual pattern. Their purpose is more pleasure and expression than power or self-defense, although a kind of power and control is achieved through both. These two patterns of mind are heavily dependent on symbolic thinking, of course. Music requires musical notation; spatial thinking requires the various symbol systems in geometry, photography, geography, painting, sculpture, and dance.

Within and across those five main patterns are the current school "disciplines." Language and mathematics, for example, are both disciplines that fall into the general pattern of "symbolic thinking" but they are different in goals, attitudes, knowledge, and skills; they still, however, share more attitudes, knowledge, and skills with one another than with spatial thinking.

These five patterns of mind help us to organize and store information and to solve problems. The better the mind can find, make, remember, and use relationships among items in the external world the better it thinks. Dave, like Andy, is judged intelligent or stupid on the quality and quantity of his patterns of mind and how these patterns influence his ability to learn. What connections can he make? How well can he remember? How well does he use information to accomplish goals and solve problems?

However, intelligence is not a uniform capacity for all knowledge. Different combinations of knowledge, skills, and attitudes result in different types of intelligence. In schools, intelligence is usually measured by the amount and level of knowledge recalled and the rapidity of skills demonstrated. Musical intelligence, though, is measured by a different kind of information remembered than "academic" intelligence.

Intelligence in U. S. history, as well as intelligence in other social studies, English, and the sciences, is measured by "academic" thinking and "symbolic" thinking. By those standards, Dave is bound to be stupid. His intelligence is judged by the "speed" of his mental actions and skills—how quickly he learns concepts and how quickly he solves problems. For Anna, understanding the concept of "capitalism" is virtually simultaneous to the explanation; she's considered brilliant in social studies because she has years of experience with picking out the various elements of government and economy; she knows, she would say "intuitively," the difference between "government" and "economy" from years of reading the newspaper. She understands the fine distinctions among words and habitually applies her understanding to her life. Dave? Capitalism is almost meaningless to him; it's a definition with virtually no referents. Is he stupid? Or simply inexperienced in academic and symbolic patterns of thinking?

Dave's intelligence in "academics" is also gauged by how early in his life he acquires certain concepts. He is considered "slow" if he is not "on grade level," that is, if he hasn't learned certain skills and knowledge by the same time as most other children. Clearly this development is related to the physical growth of his central nervous system. The ability to read, for example, depends on the development of a myelin sheath which grows from the back to the front of the brain. However, it also depends on experience. Dave may not be "slow" at all; he may just be running down a different path.

We do not know for certain whether Dave's intelligence can be significantly altered in school, but then we don't really know what intelligence is. Maybe some people are born with special talents or raised in an environment that nurtures the pattern. Certainly, either genetics or culture or both influenced the Bachs. Obviously teachers cannot influence genetic heritage, growth, or physical condition. However, we can influence the child's environment, six hours day. We certainly can change observable performance considerably by teaching the different patterns of thinking explicitly.

The rest of this book focuses on only one of those patterns: academic thinking. I've called it "academic" with some hesitation. I considered calling it "logical," "scientific," "critical," "analytic," "formal," and "logico-mathematical." Originally I preferred "philosophic" thinking because this pattern of mind focuses on thought itself. But "philosophic" doesn't emphasize its adherence to logical and empirical reasoning. "Logical," however, doesn't work because common sense has its own logic. "Scientific" and "logico-mathematical" are wrong because academic thinking is the basis of history, some psychology and sociology, and some literary and art criticism. "Scientific" also implies the pure empiricism and rationalism of the scientific revolution; academic thinking is often objective and experimental, but it is much more interactional and pragmatic than science in the eighteenth and nineteenth centuries.

"Academic" is both the best and worst choice. By sixth grade, it is the thinking pattern that not only characterizes schools but also is favored in evaluating students. Academic thinking must be taught. It must be taught better than it is now since, combined wth symbolic thinking, it best allows citizens to participate freely and equally in a Western democracy.

However, if my choice of words implies in any way that academic thinking is the "correct" thinking pattern, that it is the standard by which children should be judged intelligent and successful, then "academic" is a very poor choice. Children come to school with a variety of thinking patterns that develop from a combination of genetic heritage, nutrition, environment, and opportunity. They can all, however, acquire, improve, and exploit all five patterns of mind. Adults need access to all thinking patterns. Anna and Dave and all our children should have a chance to develop all kinds of intelligences and see the connections among them. At one end of the continuum lies a world of isolated physical elements; in the middle a variety of interconnecting patterns; and at the other end conceivably is Gregory Bateson's vision, all existence comprehended through "one pattern which connects" the living and nonliving, mankind and nature (1979).

Chapter Five

Academicwise
Academic Patterns of Mind

I am always distressed by the expression "streetwise"; it's often used by people who are NOT streetwise, and it's often said with a mixture of contempt, admiration and fear.

"Streetwise" should mean expert in living on the streets; it should mean expert in common sense. It's used incorrectly most of the time to apply to kids who survive in the street—mostly by bungling—just as "expert" often is used incorrectly to mean people who happen onto a discovery or who somehow acquire a Ph.D. Andy McGrath is often called "streetwise," not because he is smart, but because he is, somehow, "too slick."

A truly streetwise kid would know the accumulated ideas and methods of the streets; he would know street psychology and street sociology and street law and street language. -Wise means familiarity and facility with the goals, assumptions, content, and methods of any pattern of thinking. To him, the street would be like the chemist's lab is to a chemist, a place where he was expert. He could solve problems quickly by eliminating unlikely explanations and unprofitable actions. He could learn efficiently by building on his expert preconceptions. But there are few truly streetwise kids because "the school of hard knocks" is metaphorical. Andy, Dave, and our other kids on the street must learn by trial and error. Their options to improve their common sense are limited.

In secondary schools, though, there are disciplines where young people can learn other patterns of mind that have been "tried out" by earlier generations. Through history, science, English, and music, they should be able to acquire other patterns of thought useful in our society and have a chance to become academicwise, musicwise, artwise, and symbolwise.

One of these patterns, academic sense, dominates our schools and permeates the courses we consider the "core": social studies, sciences, English, and mathematics. Academic attitudes and skills are explicit in the sciences and in math; they are inexplicit, if essential, in social studies and English. In English, acquiring vocabulary and learning writing/speaking conventions involves symbolic thinking; however, writing well also requires academic logic, social development from egocentric to allocentric (a sense of audience), and an attitude of detachment from the text (to accomplish purposeful revision). Reading well involves objectivity and analysis. Academic reasoning is essential to genuine success in school.

Mr. Jenkins is one of the most popular teachers I know, particularly with "average" and "below-average" students. He's a fill-in-the-blank man. Basically, all that his students do is read short passages from his history textbook and fill in the blanks at the end of each section. His multiple choice tests come from the publisher. His class is popular because he meets many of the students' needs. He gives them stability and predictability; their goals, responsibilities, and achievements are quite clear. In fact, he meets all of their common-sense expectations. They never disappoint him; nor he them.

But they have other needs. For them, history is a content area, not a discipline; and world history is a muddle of isolated facts. Although they feel liked and comfortable in his class, they do not feel competent. Mr. Jenkins' class is not unusual. All over the country children in similar lower track classes get "skills" exercises and short reading assignments with "How well do you remember?" questions at the end—unfortunately, because these are exactly the students who need academic concept development.

Some students, when they are inundated with information, internalize the pattern of the discipline even though it is inexplicit. Like Anna, they already have acquired, somehow, the attitudes, knowledge, and skills to comprehend and recompose information without the teacher's help. We call them smart. The others, like Andy, Dave, and even Don, find no pattern; instead they live in hopelessly-jumbled "academic" minds; and we, mistakenly, assume that their heads are empty, disengaged, or "just average" rather than merely messy and undeveloped. No wonder they're sometimes bored and disgusted. We feed them information they can't digest. They don't know how.

Like Don, Mr. Jenkins' students will survive his history course, but they will not become historywise. Mr. Jenkins has failed to help them accomplish a primary goal of school: to learn to discover, create, transmit, and use our culture's coherent patterns of structuring and perceiving the world. He's given them all the necessary data. But not helping students organize this information in their own minds is as bad as not teaching at all. For students like Anna, coherence is motivation and reward; for Dave, isolated facts are not.

There's really nothing wrong with the particular knowledge that Mr. Jenkins gives out. If anyone asked me, "What information do you teach in history and science?" I'd probably give just about the same answers as most teachers in the other 15,000 districts in the country. I'd say, in general, history studies human events in the past and science investigates quantifiable phenomena in the physical world; history looks at contexts and science isolates from contexts. For more specific information, I'd go to my various curriculum guides. The state, sometimes my local board of education, and often my department explicitly list concepts students should acquire: in biology, for example, random variations; in American history, immigration; in English, the novel.

Like Mr. Jenkins, most of us stop there. We know what we have to teach. However, we don't know what the students have to learn. In high school, we don't consider what we used to call, for young children, "readiness." What a student already knows is probably the most important influence on how much and how well he learns. All ideas, including knowledge concepts, are individual. Some concepts are also public and shared. Public and shared concepts are collected in dictionaries, encyclopedias, textbooks, and curriculum guides. Teaching this public information is the primary interest of schools. However, to be valuable, memorable, and useful, public knowledge must be connected and reconnected, conceived and reconceived in each student's own mind. A student with mostly commonsense preconceptions may lack general or abstract concepts to connect new information to or may lack logical classes or structural relations or principles to connect concepts. Inappropriate preconceptions make getting additional information a torment for Andy and Dave.

Preconceptions determine perception, recognition, understanding, and memory. "All culture and all communication," Gombrich says, "depend on the interplay between expectation and observation, the waves of fulfillment, disappointment, right guesses, and wrong moves that make up our daily life" (1965, 64). Learning, in other words, is not just sensory recording of what is "out there." Dave and Andy encounter a baffling and frustrating whirl of detail in every academic class.

A person always starts with many hypotheses. When my children were small, my husband and I were walking with them along in a field in mid-Missouri:

Richard: Are those swallows?

Joan: Crows, but they have white wings.

Julia (age 7) That's why they have *scare*crows (pointing to the scarecrow).

Christopher (age 10) *That's* why they're scarecrows. They *scare* crows!

Julia: You didn't know that?

Christopher: Yeah. I knew it; I just never thought about it.

Richard: I think they're blackbirds, anyway.

All four of us had a preconception of "bird"; the creatures we saw matched it in varying degrees. Richard started with a more specialized idea, "swallow." As we got closer, those particular birds didn't fit his swallow subcategory, however, so he asked the question. Joan had "crow" which *did* fit, although, until this experience, "white wings" were not part of it. Her idea changed to accommodate the new data since all other aspects of the birds fit "crows." She, in fact, reconceptualized (or, in Piagetian words, "accommodated") her concept.

The children, of course, were also developing a variety of academic preconceptions in this interchange: about birds, crows, swallows, blackbirds, and scarecrows, but they were also constructing attitudes about the function of language, intellectual risk-taking, and word play. Finally, they were practicing academic skills such as labeling, hypothesizing, analyzing, and connecting.

Other families would have had totally different conversations, even if they had finally identified the birds the same way—different humor, different approach to the topic, different relationship of adults to children. Maybe they would have been in a zoo, not a field. Maybe they would have thrown rocks. Everyone's children come to school with preconceptions: mature, immature; inappropriate, appropriate; commonsense, academic; American, Japanese; Midwestern, Northeastern. Maturity in academic disciplines, however, requires understanding and at least tolerating basic academic assumptions.

Although the knowledge that we all teach is usually explicit and shared, academic attitudes are hidden. In order to teach these attitudes, we must articulate them:

1. value for **active, deliberate, persistent, flexible** effort to find the "truth"

2. toleration for **ambiguity** and **relativity**

3. sense of **detachment** and **allocentrism**

Of these three, the most important academic attitude is "detachment." Detachment doesn't mean exactly the same in each of the

disciplines. In literature we expect detachment with empathy; we
want students both to see the text as an artifact, created by an author's
choices, and also to believe in the characters. That attitude is extremely complex, much more difficult than most English teachers
(who are already good critics) recognize. Sean, in my eleventh grade
once, burst out in sincere terror during class about *Winesburg, Ohio:*
"If that _ _ _ _ _ _ _ [a character in the novel] touches me, I'll change
his face with a tire iron." In literature, we expect empathy, but
just enough. In science, we want detachment without empathy or
connection.

A highly refined attitude of detachment is what, in the last few
years, cognitive psychologists mean by the catch-word "metacognition." Metacognition means thinking about thinking, knowing, as
Roger Brown says, what you know, when you need to know it, and
how to change your knowlege. Minding the mind is one step beyond
awareness of your writing style or your experimental method; it is
awareness of your own mind as it interacts with physical, moral,
social, and symbolic behavior. Mr. Jenkins is cheating his students if
he does not explicitly teach them detachment, as well as toleration
for ambiguity and relativity and value for persistence in finding
"truth."

Students also arrive at our classes with or without appropriate
academic skills and methods. When mental actions are combined
into intentional or conscious patterns of thinking, we call them skills:
analyzing, synthesizing, inferring, interpreting, judging, applying,
and predicting, for example. The scientific method and deductive
reasoning are patterns of skills. So are reading and writing.

Each pattern of mind has its own set of appropriate methods.
Academic thinking uses logical rules of inquiry: inductive, deductive, analogical, and syllogistic reasoning, for example. Other cognitive patterns like musical thinking, spatial thinking, and symbolic
thinking have different rules. Academic sense also emphasizes
"higher order thinking skills." What people often mean by higher
order is Bloom's last four levels of reasoning: application, analysis,
synthesis, and evaluation (1956). These logical methods and analytic
skills are often quite different from commonsense strategies.

While these particular methods of inquiry characterize all "academics," different disciplines emphasize different parts of the logical
processes. Induction and deduction, for example, are different parts
of the same logical process. Science is primarily (though not exclu-
sivly) deductive; it starts from the general and moves to the specific.
The hypothesis is the beginning and tests that don't disprove the
hypothesis are the result. Science focuses on elaborate testing of the

hypothesis; the process for coming up with hypotheses receives less emphasis. Prediction is specifying other examples that will also support the hypothesis.

History emphasizes the other half, induction to find a central principle or hypothesis. Of course, historiographers claim that, because historians operate within a culture, they begin with cultural hypotheses, perhaps more so than scientists; and, of course, historians from Herodotus to Hollinshed and Halévy differ enormously in logical processes. However, in simple terms, the elements in history *are* the context—not items to be isolated as in science. The specifics are the beginning and the hypothesis the conclusion. The historian looks for positive proof, although hypotheses are not always provable; they are much more like guesses. Observation is "armchair" observation, introspection rather than inspection, recollection rather than collection. The tools of a historian are human artifacts rather than physical implements for observing and measuring. A historian's tools are found rather than designed. Prediction is by analogous principles and examples.

To be good in high school academic courses, students must rigorously apply "logical reasoning" skills. To be good in high school science they must be able to work from the abstract to the particular; in history they must be able to abstract and sort from the details. In general, the historic method is intuitive, analogical and metaphorical; the scientific method is physical and concrete, although there are exceptions. History is holistic, science atomistic; the historian is Miss Marple, the scientist Sherlock Holmes.

Both Miss Marple and Sherlock Holmes are mysterious to Dave. He hasn't learned the reasoning skills that inductive and deductive reasoning require; analysis and synthesis, for example. Concepts grow through mental actions. While there is no development in mental actions, there is development in those intellectual skills that combine and apply mental actions to new content. Development in these skills means increasing their automaticity, rapidity, and simultaneity.

Learning ping pong isn't very different from learning literary analysis. When Anna or Dave start to learn ping pong, they already have the basic hand-eye coordination necessary; it's automatic and unconscious. However, the specific content and skills are new. Anna and Dave first concentrate on hitting the ball; then they work on other parts of the game—getting the ball over the net, gauging where the ball will land on the opponent's side of the table, guessing where the other player is least likely to hit it, and, finally, making distracting, smart-aleck remarks. Sooner or later, for experts, all those actions happen quickly, simultaneously, and automatically—except perhaps the smart mouth. Learning to read a book critically or to analyze the forces that led to World War II requires the same kind of practice.

Some theorists claim that unconscious pratice is best. Students should use the scientific method, solve math problems, or analyze literature without reflecting on these processes. The various "slotting and expansion" programs in English are *unconscious* practice. Others emphasize *consciousness* of the process. If the ping-pong player consciously reflects on his stroke, he is thinking about playing. Instrumental Enrichment (Feuerstein 1980), Whimbey's problem solving methods (1982), and Philosophy for Children (Lipman 1980) all emphasize awareness of thought processes. However, whether we emphasize unconscious practice or teach metacognition, we must teach academic reasoning explicitly if Dave is ever going to learn.

Academic generalization, for example, is hard for Dave. In most commonsense situations, quick generalization made on few variables is customary. We assume that the nurse we hire to stay with our aged mother is reliable. We get her name from an approved agency and we usually don't look for much evidence to disprove our theory that she's reliable because we have to act quickly in an emergency. Similarly, police officers move quickly when they hear an alarm and see two men running from a store. Sometimes, of course, quick generalization doesn't work in everyday situations at all. When he was seven, my son Christopher tried to wade in a gulley and was swept into a sewer because he assumed that water is consistently calm all the way down. Overgeneralization is never appropriate in science courses though. Dave refuses to consider life of any sort on any other planets; for him, all life has all the qualities he knows right here on earth. Dave consistently undergeneralizes too. In algebra, he can't solve any problem if it isn't identical to the example in his text: he can't find the overall principle in the solution. We must help Dave learn to generalize and particularize.

We also ought to help him practice structuring ideas so he will know how things fit together. He can't understand biology if he cannot structure hierachically. What are the parts of living things? What are living things part of? What are living things logically equivalent to? He has to practice putting things in a variety of orders: temporal, spatial, cause/effect, form/function, or comparison and contrast.

These skills, combined with appropriate attitudes, might begin to allow students like Dave and Don to acquire the knowledge and facts which Mr. Jenkins handed out so futilely. However, even with academic skills and attitudes, students also need appropriate knowledge preconceptions. Andrea A. diSessa describes how knowledge preconceptions influence understanding in physics. In her research diSessa proposed the following problem:

> If a steel ball is dropped, it picks up speed and kinetic energy. When the ball hits the floor, however, it stops (before bouncing up again). At that instant, there is no kinetic energy since there is no motor. Where did the energy go? (1981)

A physicist knows: the ball and the floor are mutually compressing on impact. That compression, just like the compression of a spring, stores energy in mechanical distortion. That's where the energy goes when the ball comes to a stop. The distortion pushes the ball back up into the air. However, in diSessa's research, beginners wouldn't even accept "springiness" as an explanation when it was offered. In the ordinary world, hard things are *not* springy. Tennis balls bounce, but glass and steel are, by common sense, rigid. Physicists, on the other hand, know that springiness is a much more probable explanation than rigidity. A physicist knows this principle unconsciously and eliminates explanations that students, equipped only with common sense, can't. Students must try many more possible choices than someone who is physics-wise. They are like little Christopher with the yellow, red, and blue Tupperware. Our students are not absolute novices, however; they *have* already developed some preconceptions about what choices are likely in scientific situations. They certainly know that the explanation is highly unlikely to be "act of God" or "hatred of the ball for floors." In other cultures at other times, either of those explanations could be viable.

In each class, we are trying to develop expertise, i.e., appropriate knowledge to prepare the child for the next conceptual level. Development is going from partially knowing, when most answers seem valid, to knowing what answers are probable. In order for those sixteen-year-olds to become wise, they must develop appropriate preconceptions, not just memorize isolated data.

Students don't need any particular one set of concepts to understand your course, but they do need certain kinds of preconceptions. In biology, for example, DNA and cell make little sense without the concept "living things." "Cat" may seem a long way from DNA but when he pats his first kitty, a child has taken a first step toward the conceptual maturity of a biologist. Between that first pat and his first biology test, the child may have lived Dave's life or Anna's—or Julia's, Andy's, or Don's. He may have set "ball" bugs on fire or carefully carried spiders outside because he treasured Charlotte in *Charlotte's Web;* he may even have mugged old people for their welfare checks or he might have voluteered to feed and clothe the homeless. If the student does NOT develop the many preconceptions that might build a mature conception of living things, it is useless for the teacher to ask him to memorize a definition of cell.

DNA, cell and living thing are ideas that can be composed from a variety of preconceptions. However, two powerful, basic preconceptions are essential to every academic discipline: time and space. Piaget (1954), Moffett (1968), Kohlberg (1972), Guilford (1957), and Bloom (1956) all describe development in terms of understanding time and space.

Denny started me thinking about time. Denny was a seventeen-year-old, "above average" student in the first history class I ever taught. He dutifully took notes, read his assignments, answered questions in class, and made *B*'s on tests. When I announced that the final, three weeks away, would indeed cover Egypt, 2000 B.C. to the present, he came in after school and burst into tears.

"You've understood it all year, Denny. Just review."

"There's no time to study!"

"Three weeks?"

It turned out that Denny felt he had to reread the entire text twice and rememorize every single date. He had no idea that:

- 2000 B.C. was 4000 years ago
- 4000 years is approximately 200 generations
- history is about change over time
- historical periods might have distinguishable characteristics
- historical events occurred in Egypt, China, and North America simultaneously

He had been memorizing—quite well—disconnected facts. He had no sense of the story at all. The raw information just jostled around in his mind. Denny isn't at all unusual. Many adolescents, like Denny, don't have appropriate preconceptions about time. (Hallam 1970; Zaccaria 1978).

Space is another of the first ideas children explore. They begin to study three-dimensional space (and geology) when they play peek-a-boo and then hide-and-seek. However, by the time they get to adolescence, many students can't really imagine countries on the other side of the planet. North and south? Very few high school students really have a concept of direction; and fourteen degrees north longitude is absolute nonsense. Mercator projections? For many students, the map really is the actual territory—a flat map at that.

Yet time and space are the basic organizational structures for social studies, sciences and mathematics. History is about change over time; global studies about the influence of time and space on culture. Geologic time is necessary for earth science (most teenagers do not even comprehend the idea of fifty years, much less a million). Biology and geometry obviously depend on spatial organization.

Concepts of time and space also underly the other structural concepts: part/whole or cause/effect, for example. Causality is change over time; part/whole is relationships in space; form/function is space and time; equality is derived from space. All those structural concepts are necessary to academic wisdom. How can Andy learn the laws of motion if he doesn't understand causality?

A young child lives in the present place. At first she names and identifies—"milk." Then she states in the here and now—"Milk all gone." Slowly she learns what happened yesterday in the next block; her parents were children before her time and her teacher lives in a house, not the school room. The way the children conceive time after that depends on their experiences. Years ago at dinner my son Christopher would start with a line like "the most excellent thing happened to Conan the Barbarian" and then he'd retell the entire plot of the book rather than explain the "excellent thing." He wasn't comfortable leaving chronological sequence for logical exposition. He still tells a good tale, but he has also learned to "get to the point" when "getting to the point" is appropriate.

Narration certainly can be developed into a fine art; Dave is a masterful storyteller. So is Anna. Narration and description are highly valued in commonsense communication; logical exposition is highly valued in academic environments. If Dave is to be successful in U. S. history, he must also learn logical structures of cause/effect and part/whole.

A child not only builds the specific concepts of each discipline, but he must also develop more mature concepts, closer to the understanding of the experts. A high school biology student's idea of "cat" must mature from the child's to the expert biologist's. Academic concepts mature in three ways: they depend less and less on sensory perception; they become more specific and more general; and they become more orderly.

As children's thinking matures, less perceptible concepts are accessible to them. Some concepts, like "DNA," have physical attributes but students still can't actually see DNA; others, like "gravity" don't even have any physical qualities. DNA and gravity are virtually inaccessible to Dave and Don. By high school, Dave has to learn almost entirely through words rather than concrete things or actions. When he studies the "world view" of the Chinese, his teacher can demonstrate it partially by getting a guest speaker to show the class the "tea ceremony" or calligraphy, but most learning in high school occurs through words. Although science laboratories are a little more experiential, they still depend on words and other symbol systems. How can Dave and Don, who haven't already built a ladder from the sensory to the general and abstract, now learn the abstract concepts at a totally symbolic level? How will they ever learn to conceive like experts?

Experts in any field—biology, physics, or history (or bridge, for that matter)—have bigger chunks of information filled with more specifics and glued together with larger generalities. The more general the concept, the more useful in learning. A successful student becomes more successful because she doesn't have to learn every isolated instance; she can fit new examples into existing structures and eliminate irrelevant information. Anna has spent fifteen years reading biographies and historical novels; she's read *Little House on the Prairie* repeatedly. She reads the paper and watches educational television. She has a context for every new piece of information in U. S. history; she can connect it with individuals, clothing and architecture, and events. She also finds more and more specific examples the more she reads; each detail fits neatly into her categories; unconsciously, she even cross references by time, space, and cause and effect. What Dave must memorize, Anna simply absorbs and integrates. As they get older, the gap between Dave and Anna becomes proportionally, even astronomically, greater and greater.

Learning is restructuring concepts about the internal and external world. By the time a child is in high school, there are no totally new ideas; that is, every concept is based on many preconceptions. Maybe students encounter a familiar instance of a preconception and assimilate it into the idea: that's recognition, elaboration, or specification. Maybe they encounter an instance which doesn't quite fit (as Joan did with the crow's white wings). Then, they restructure or "accommodate" the preconception to fit the discontinuity. Successful education is composing old ideas and new experiences into new patterns. Some of those patterns we call knowledge, attitudes, and skills; some of them we call history, sociology, physics, chemistry, and biology. Some we call common sense or academic sense. Some we call "Newtonian thought" or "organic" thought (Capra 1982). Whatever we call them, these patterns partly determine the way we see the world and ourselves.

Fritjof Capra claims our world is in crisis because of the pattern we use to see it. He blames our "scientific" world view for pollution, inflation, unemployment, the energy crisis, the health care crisis, violence, and crime. That "analytic" or "rational" pattern perceives the universe as a mechanical system; its goal is to measure and categorize. It includes the ideas of rugged individualism and competition, unlimited progress through economics and technology, and human control of the natural world (1982).

Since Copernicus, Kepler, Bacon, and Newton, our Western world view has certainly been "scientific." Bacon's inductive empiricism combined with Descartes' deductive rationalism were the basis of the scientific revolution, the industrial revolution, and the Enlightenment. Our democratic ideals as well as our public educational system grew from these roots. Locke thought that freedom and equality were natural laws similar to Newton's physical laws; those "inalienable rights" still constitute our national philosophy. Jefferson's belief in an educated populace is the basis of our educational ideology.

Capra contrasts this rational pattern to the world view we associate with Asian cultures: Hindus, Buddhists, Taoists, for example. In an "ecological," or "organic" world view, he says, knowledge comes through expanded states of awareness; "spirit" is a mode of consciousness. The individual feels connected to the entire cosmos. This thinking pattern is the opposite of analytic: nonlinear, holistic, and synthesizing. It's based on the "essential interrelatedness and interdependence of all phenomena—physical, biological, psychological, social and cultural."

According to Capra, we need both the organic patterns and the mechanistic view, intuition and reason, religion and science. We not only have to describe molecules but also see them as parts in a living system. Capra calls his synthesis of Western and Eastern patterns a "systems" view of life. We can only avert this profound, worldwide crisis by seeing ourselves and the world through a systems view.

This chapter is entitled "Academic Patterns of Mind," but it is also about other patterns, such as the "systems" view; its main subject is our students and the impact their patterns of mind have on them and on our society. Dave and Anna both live and work in my town. They graduated the same year, and neither went on to college. As I stop by the store on the way home from work, I hear a yell in the Shop Rite parking lot, "Hey, you don't even say 'Hi'?" It's Dave, driving the same kind of truck he drove when he was seventeen. He's a decent, friendly, generous, loyal, and hard-working man, but he doesn't have the resources that Anna does. He can't choose to think academically. There are books he can't read and feelings he can't express effectively. Every once in a while, he and some of his classmates take me out to lunch. We talk about our lives. Dave is often bored with his. When he has personal or social problems, his internal resources for dealing with them are limited: he is frustrated at mistreatment by the government, the rich, and his boss. I like Dave; and

I feel sad, maybe even guilty, that he has been cheated of something he didn't even know he had.

Surviving in secondary school, like survival on the streets, doesn't show that graduates are wise. It only shows that they have survived. The number of survivors, the percentage of students who graduate, is not the significant statistic. When we teach children academic disciplines, we're teaching powerful ways to understand and enjoy the world. School is the most likely place for Dave to learn academic patterns; yet for him and other students, academic thinking alone is quite restrictive. An educated adult must be able to view the same event through a variety of patterns. Each pattern constructs a piece of truth. Dave's common sense constructs one piece; Anna's academic sense and her symbolic sense construct another. In addition, Anna has the curiosity and the intellectual resources to learn about other patterns. She's already fascinated with Native Americans, ancient Greece and Rome, ancient and modern Asian thought, and current Western religious/spiritual thought. Someday, she will be able to understand non-Western and ancient patterns of mind as well.

What is truly important is not how many of our students survive, but what percentage of the survivors know the streets *and* the laboratory. What percentage are streetwise *and* academicwise? What percentage have access to continued learning? Additional patterns? What percentage have multiple pathways to wisdom?

Chapter Six

Dog Killing in the Philippines
Teaching Academic Thinking

Teaching thinking begins in the teacher's mind; but learning thinking occurs in students' minds; so there are two basic tasks for teachers—identifying where seniors should be in June and discovering where each student is now. All of our other choices simply involve helping students get from here to there.

Laura wrote "Dog Killing in the Phillipines," early in her senior year to submit to a local paper. She felt passionate about the topic and was eager to get my help so she could incite others to feel outraged about what was happening to dogs (see Figure 6–1).

There are some simple questions you can always ask yourself to understand where a student is now in terms of skills, knowledge and attitudes:

1. How would you describe Laura's academic thinking skills? Does she see the parts of the situation? Compare? Organize? Work from logical premises? Draw appropriate conclusions?

2. What kind of information does she seem to have? About the economy of the Philippines? The U. S. economy? The government?

3. Does she use the appropriate academic vocabulary? What do you think she generally reads? What newspaper, for example?

4. Would you guess that her attitudes toward learning in school are primarily those we connect with academic sense or with common

53

Figure 6-1

In the Phillipines President Marcos is letting innocent dog killings go on. The people in the Phillipines are cruelly killing and torturing their dogs. The reason is not that they are hungry or anything like that. Its just that dog meat is considered a delicacy.

For Christmas I got two little puppies. I could never do anything that they do to their animals. Dogs have emotions and feelings just as humans do except dogs can't talk.

Laura McPherson
Grade 12

---

sense? Is she precise? Thorough? Objective? Is she analytic or intuitive? Flexible or rigid? How persistently did she work on this piece of writing? What did she do to improve it?

5. What about her personal attitudes? Would you guess she is socially mature? Confident?

At first it seems that Laura can't even identify the parts of this situation; she doesn't seem to distinguish among the "people," the "president," and the government. However, a fundamental problem is that she has launched into a totally unfamiliar topic; all she knows is what she read in *The Star*. She doesn't even know there *are* parts. This content void partially necessitates her final desperate assertion about dogs' emotions. Feelings she *does* know about, even though she has precious little hard data on dogs' feelings. Her major illogical classification of "how they treat dogs" as parallel to "how I treat my puppy" involves a confusion of logical types. The behavior of a government toward animals that are potential food is parallel to the behavior of another government. Does the United States permit the inhumane production and marketing of any meat? Veal? Of course, calves aren't so cuddly as puppies but Laura, because she is unaware of veal production, cannot begin to see the fallacy in her comparison.

Laura can't even structure her own thought hierarchically. She has mastered the conventions of writing; the essay is comparatively "correct" in spelling, punctuation, sentence structure, and manuscript form; but a senior in high school should also have mastered the organizational skills for effective writing. Had she been able to outline the essay mentally she might have wondered "What is parallel to a business killing animals for food?" The answer isn't "The way one citizen treats her puppy."

She doesn't have the vocabulary to manipulate complex political and ethical issues either. In conference with me, she didn't know the difference between the words "slaughter" and "butcher" in reference to animals or the difference among the words "assassinate," "murder," and "massacre" in reference to people. She also didn't know "economy" at all and had no idea what concepts it might elucidate. She doesn't have the attitudes necessary for an effective argument either. She isn't able to consider the possible opinions of Pilipinos. It's hard for Laura to imagine a different world view; she can't put herself in the place of anyone who is unlike her. "Different" often means weird or immoral; she told me that "everyone knows that eating dog is disgusting and cruel." She assumes that the author of the article she read, like Laura, is simply incensed at the cruelty; she never suspects the paper might be exploiting her feelings for profit. She isn't self-critical enough to ask if people in her country behave similarly; and she isn't flexible enough to modify her opinion. In fact, in a typically commonsense way, she uses all the logic at her disposal to justify her original opinion.

Laura was, however, quite persistent. She chose the topic herself and spent considerable time rewriting. She came to me even though the paper was not assigned in my class; she also conferred several times with her English teacher and discussed it at least once with her science teacher. However, she couldn't benefit much from the four long conversations she and I had about this paper. For her, revising meant recopying. She thought in terms of "errors"; there was right information that I must know as a social studies teacher, and, after I gave it to her, she could copy it down. She couldn't think of herself as having the intellectual resources to accomplish her goals. She was unable to consider the text as an artifact and ask "What should I chose to do to this text to make it more provocative?" She ended up feeling frustrated, helpless and inadequate. So did I.

The next question is obvious:

6. Is Laura able to complete the task with the attitudes, knowledge, and skills she seems to have?

The answer is equally obvious: no, not if the task is to write a convincing, publishable editorial. I could teach her more about the government, politics, and economy of the United States and the Philippines. I also could help her find other relevant news articles, maybe the arguments of animal rights activists who agreed with her or representatives of the meat industry who disagreed; but she would have to build knowledge other students had been acquiring for eighteen years. I also know many ways she could practice connecting and organizing new information. Even then, she still would have commonsense attitudes that block her acquiring, structuring and using information. Everything Laura knows consciously and unconsciously tells her that she should act on her "gut feeling." It also, unfortunately, tells her that additional information will just muddy the water. I think Laura and I both knew that the answer was no.

Laura actually graduated from high school five months after she wrote "Dog Killing"; her diploma should have shown that she had mastered the skills, knowledge, and attitudes that she needed. Certainly after my government class as well as courses in economics, global studies, U. S. history, and English, Laura should have had the tools to meet her goals. She didn't. Laura couldn't even begin to have significant impact on her world.

A healthy, effective citizen must be able to be informed, skilled, committed, and active. Skills and knowledge are useless without commitment and action. Laura has the passionate commitment that often ignites great accomplishment; she also, at eighteen, still energetically works to make changes. However, a citizen who is active and committed without knowledge and skills is dangerous. Laura is potentially dangerous. She's frustrated and angry with the people in the Philippines. In her world, right and wrong are traditional, clear, and unquestionable. Puppies are precious members of the household; and feelings are separate from, and more important than, ideas. A culture that eats puppies threatens her entire value system. The Pilipinos are evil because they are unknown, and, for her, at this stage of her life, unknowable. She hasn't been empowered through history or science or literature to understand them. She will probably never know those people, not through television, not through travel, not through books, because she also hasn't learned to value learning.

"If only," Solzhenitsyn says, "there were evil people somewhere insidiously committing evil deeds and it were necessary only to separate them from the rest of us and destroy them. But the line dividing good and evil cuts through the heart of every human being and who is willing to destroy a piece of his own heart?" (1974). Unfortunately she has never heard of Solzhenitsyn and is unable to envision the heart that she shares with Pilipino people.

Changing Students by What You Teach

Only one question remains; unfortunately, no one asked it soon enough for Laura:

7. How would you teach Laura enough that she could complete the tasks required of an effective citizen, a productive worker, a healthy family member, a contributing member of her society, and a satisified individual?

The first steps, of course, are to decide what citizens should be able to do and to develop authentic assessments that test their ability to meet those real-world goals. Then, in the classroom, the teacher must help students build the necessary attitudes, knowledge, and skills. Up until now, our major emphasis in school has been wrong: we have focused on acquisition of knowledge, rather than use; on breadth of data, rather than depth of personal understanding; and on information alone, rather than information, skills, and attitudes together.

Ironically, what Laura wants to do herself is a good example of the kind of authentic assessment she should have had in her many social studies classes. All citizens ought to be able to choose a public issue from the newspaper (exactly what she did do); then, using history and culture studies, they should be able to analyze the issue, come to a reasoned position, and argue effectively (exactly what she could *not* do).

Laura's difficulty, and the problem for fifty to seventy per cent of our students, is that she was allowed to "get by with "solid *C*'s" in her classes. She really couldn't *do* much all along beyond "school" assignments. She had ability and worked hard. She could fill in the blank; she remembered enough details and recognized enough textual clues for multiple choice. She could memorize a short definition and remember information long enough to take a test. Her nearly flawless manuscript form was useless, however, without content; her test-taking skills and short-term memory were superfluous in the adult world where the real tests are what you can do.

There is no point in simply "giving" Laura more definitions, this time of "economy" or "production and distribution." Generally students, and some teachers, believe in our day-to-day thinking that ideas are "out there." "Economy" (as well as "D Day," and *Roe vs. Wade*) exists as an entity that we must "get through our heads." It really isn't. While the definition of "economy" is standard, the actual concept in a particular mind involves many unique characteristics. The structure must be created by Laura's own preconceptions and perceptions. After we choose our key concepts carefully, and sparingly, we must help our students incorporate them into their understanding.

The key concepts of a discipline are the main ideas, the concepts that the leaders in the field agree either explicitly or tacitly are essential. "Democracy" is obviously a key concept in U. S. history and government. There are also key subconcepts: the *Bill of Rights,* the revolution, and Thomas Jefferson, for example.

"Theocracy in Salem" is probably not absolutely required (although for particular groups at particular times it might be useful). Between the *Bill of Rights* and "theocracy in Salem" fall numerous bits of information that constitute the history of the United States. How many of them are absolutely essential? If you look at a typical high school textbook in almost any field (other than your own), you will be astounded at the number of formulas, theories, facts, events, dates, people, places, and ideas. Teaching thinking isn't inundating students with data but encouraging a thorough understanding of main ideas. Laura is a product of broad coverage and is, at eighteen, quite narrow.

Finally, for Laura and for other students, we have focused on the knowledge to the exclusion of attitudes and skills. They are both essential to knowledge acquisition. Laura would have been a quite different student if her preconception of democracy included the idea that "democracy only works if citizens are active, committed, skilled, and informed." She believes that "democracy means everybody has a right to his own opinion." Opinion, for her, means "gut feeling."

In the same way, her skills are part of her concept of economy. Teaching conceptualizing is teaching students *to do.* Of course, Laura will be unable to understand the U. S. and Philippine economy if she does not have enough information to see what the parts of a national economy are; she obviously needs to memorize certain facts. Memorization, however, usually implies recollecting specific data or definitions. In twelve years of public school, Laura has been exposed to enough facts to understand economy ten times over. To understand, learn, and remember, a student must fit new information into old patterns. In the adult world, real tests are based on established patterns of habits, skills, attitudes, and long-term information. Laura doesn't have those patterns.

Changing Students By Where You Teach

The important place in teaching is the student's mind; the important time is the juncture of preconception and perception. One such moment, however, does not make learning; Laura can't learn what she needs in one moment. The only way for children to form concepts is repeated practice: constant interactions of old and new ideas, methods tried and revised, attitudes encountered and changed. In the four years between ninth grade and twelfth, there are thousands of these moments of reconception. These moments make up what students are and what they believe; they help determine what sort of parents, workers, neighbors, and citizens they will be.

We can create these moments of reconception in the way we talk with our students, organize our class activities, and give our assignments. Then, unlike Laura, our students will have the opportunity to graduate, changed.

Changing Students By The Way *You* Talk

In common, everyday talk, children are told "change your attitude" or "you have an attitude." Those statements mean: "You have the wrong attitude. Take mine!" Just as racist talk encourages racism, this kind of talk represents, and encourages, a "right-answer" or "passive acceptance" model. Teachers have to demonstrate, not command, academic attitudes such as purposefulness, precision, choice, consequences, detachment, flexibility, responsibility, and confidence. Actually modeling those attitudes is fairly difficult; most of us slip into commonsense thinking patterns all the time. When a fifteen year old takes class time asking "Why can't we chew gum in class?" teachers are often more concerned with the time it takes to answer the question than the value of showing that questioning is an important skill. In theory, social studies teachers know that the gum question is as legitimate in their classroom society as "Why should we pay a tax on tea?" was in a larger society. Efficiency is not an academic value; it is a commonsense value. Yet most teachers are tempted, after twenty-five years of answering it, to cut the gum question short.

A more direct way to teach those attitudes is to develop a list of *questions to ask students;* these questions are based on academic attitudes. For example, to encourage detachment, purposefulness, precision, and choice, you can ask these questions frequently:

- Why did you choose to say . . . rather than . . . ?
- What do you intend to achieve by . . . ?

- What other ways can you think of to . . . ?
- How did you learn that . . . ?

Questions like those are useful in casual conversations, in conferences, and in marginal comments on papers; you can also ask the entire class to answer them in their learning logs or ask small groups to answer them in reference to projects or activities. The more frequently you ask, the more likely students will begin to assume that they have power to change their ideas, their thoughts, and their effectiveness.

Scaffolding is another pattern of talking with students; you help them build concepts by adding support. Scaffolding demonstrates the underlying skills, attitudes, and knowledge that allow a student to go to a more academic level of conceptualization; the verbal interchange itself entices them into practicing skills, attitudes, and language. Parents often "scaffold" for young children quite naturally. The knowledge concept is dog:

Child: See doggie.

Parent: That's a big dog, isn't it?

Child: Big doggie gone. All gone.

Parent: Where did the big dog go?

Child: All gone.

In that short conversation the parent not only modeled skills, attitudes, and language structure but also gave information. "Big dog" implies greater precision in classifying, which the child immediately imitates. "Where did the big dog go?" models speculation and also suggests the underlying concept of space. The parent also repeats in appropriate sentence structure. Never once, however, in this familiar learning situation, does the parent lecture or correct.

In scaffolding, the teacher can ask questions for additional information or repeat the idea using precise vocabulary or complex sentence structure. What the teacher does not do is impose her own ideas on the student. Scaffolding creates another instant of preconception, perception, and reconception (The concept is economy; the subconcept food production and distribution):

Teacher: You really hate the idea of hurting dogs, don't you?

Laura: My puppies are so cute. They're almost grown now.

Teacher: I don't like hurting any animals unnecessarily, do you?

Laura: Chickens are stupid and dirty. Cluck, Cluck. Cluck. Cluck. Just cluck-clucks. You don't have to hurt them, I guess.

Teacher: You think it's worse to hurt dogs?

Laura: I don't care much about chickens. If I was a vegetarian, I'd still eat chickens. They're stupid *and* ugly.

Teacher: I've heard that geese are not treated very well in this country when they are raised for goose-liver pâté.

Laura: What's that?

Teacher: Goose liver pâté? Pâté is ground-up goose liver, usually baked like a meat loaf. You sell it canned in your Shop Rite (where Laura works).

The conversation could go on. The point is not to change Laura's opinion but to give her enough information to imagine a "system of food production and distribution" in the United States. She works in a major grocery chain store; yet she is remarkably distant from that concept. Maybe she has not been forced to develop questions in classes; at least she has apparently never wondered "Where does the food in grocery stores come from? What regulations limit its production? Does the government control it?" Laura has passed a state competency test that covered the Industrial Revolution, the Meat Inspection Act, the Food and Drug Act, the New Deal, and Progressivism; yet she never connected that information in any significant way with the food she sells every day.

This conversation took less than one minute; we were walking out of the classroom. In fact, halls, doorways, and lunchrooms are three of the most effective educational environments I know. Some of your students haven't had conversations like the "big doggie" dialogue; when they said "See doggie," an adult said, "Hush up, people are staring!" or otherwise implied that verbal exploring, describing, labeling, and classifying were secondary. You want to teach a different lesson. If you store this dialogue pattern in your mind, you can pull it out, easily and painlessly, to use spontaneously on the next field trip.

Changing Students By The Way *They* Talk:

Teachers talk too much in class. We really don't need to practice talking or thinking. So why do we do all the talking and thinking? We set goals, develop strategies, organize information, evaluate learning, and discuss ideas. Sometimes, of course, teachers have to talk. Maybe they have to share some fascinating personal information that isn't in the text or perhaps it's necessary to explain a procedure; but usually the teacher's time is better spent helping students practice language and thought. Even when the teacher does have to talk, the students shouldn't be intellectually idle; they should actively think even when they're listening.

Large group discussions are unlikely to produce as much active thought as small groups. Most large group discussion isn't really discussion anyway; it's more often a test to see if a few students know the right answer or an exercise for others to avoid being called on. Every once in a while, a free-flowing, open-ended discussion with students ranging around a topic, talking simultaneously, giving personal responses, exploring, questioning, and speculating is fun. That kind of discussion is difficult to maintain. Even at its best, in a class of twenty-five, many students will be either distracted or passive. Usually, large group discussion, which characterizes most student classroom talk, is exactly the wrong way to teach academic thinking.

The familiar combination of the teacher lecturing and then asking questions is deadly to thought. When I was a high school student (and again when I first taught English), I participated in hundreds of literature classes where students sat passively while the teacher lectured on main themes, symbolism, and vocabulary; sometimes the teacher asked questions and a few students raised their hands to answer. As an adolescent I thought, if I thought about it at all, that the purpose of literature classes was to learn the names of the books and remember the plots. Sometimes, I loved the books, but I always felt guilty when I read them straight through instead of answering the study questions. Outside of class assignments, I read voraciously, and differently. So long as teenagers think that they're reading for plot and symbolism, no amount of lecture will make many of them read and understand *Grapes of Wrath* in any depth. It's a "school" book.

Small groups are totally different. Students can each talk actively. They're talking to their peers; they can argue about what the book means to them, explain how they know the meaning, and speculate about the purpose of literature. They can do all kinds of small projects together, develop a list of questions, write a letter, or create a display. Small group interactions change the students' attitudes and interests. After interacting with other students' understandings, they come to Jim Casy and Rose o' Sharon with different preconceptions.

Most in-class, small group activities, however, are short, simple, and highly structured. "Spend five minutes in pairs listing seven reasons for. . ." Students can combine writing and discussion: "Spend five minutes writing a response to . . .; then give your response to your partner. She should spend five minutes arguing with it." These little groups can be focused on almost any topic: an upcoming debate, current events, a book, or a scientific principle. In contrast to sitting still and listening, participating in these small groups provokes multiple intersections of preconception, perception, and reconception.

Short, simple, structured groups are easy to establish. Long, complex group activities are difficult to sustain if you don't have a classroom pattern of taking group activities seriously. You should always start a class on group work with pairs of students and with highly circumscribed activities. Later, when you know your group and also your own skills and tolerances, you can expand the size of the groups and the scope of the activities. Then you're free to observe.

Once small group processes are established, they can be wonderfully flexible. You can have several small group activities in a period, alternating perhaps with your explanations, student presentations, reading, or writing. Students can be stopped and put into groups any time you feel that they're not actively engaged. It's important, however, to remember that the point of small group activities is individual thinking and learning. Occasionally, "collaborative" or "cooperative" learning becomes fashionable again. In those periods we tend to forget that the small group activity is not the point in itself.

Changing Students By The Way They Write

Whatever else is happening in the classroom, lecture, large group discussion, or small group activities, the student should be actively thinking. Having every student writing is the best way to keep every student thinking. All language-making is thinking-making. Language doesn't just label or mirror ideas; it remakes them. As soon as students must use words, they must make their concepts more precise and more general, simultaneously. To choose words, students must differentiate, categorize, organize, generalize, and specify. Only by reading, writing, and using the word "economy" in multiple contexts can Laura begin to know that it means more than "something like not spending a lot."

In small groups, more students talk; so more students must think. However, listening and speaking happen fast, much too fast to be recalled and reconsidered most of the time. Written-down language is thought written down. You can see the students' thoughts in their writing and so can they; you can ask them to revise their thoughts and they can see what needs revision. Also writing is constantly active. It's difficult to daydream and write simultaneously. Much academic learning should happen through writing. I worry whenever I talk more than five minutes without requiring students to make some kind of active individual written response; I want be sure they're listening with their minds as well as with their ears.

Of course, high school teachers have always relied on notetaking. Notes are especially useful to teach generalizing, summarizing, and remembering. In addition to traditional class notes, though, I like to use focused free-writing, double-entry notes, learning logs, word webs, and lists. None of these forms is particularly new; what's innovative is the extent to which they can be used. These five simple strategies can keep each student actively practicing academic skills during the period. I instantly know who isn't participating because their pencils aren't moving; and if I'm worried that someone doesn't understand, I can wander over during class and read that one student's writing. Writing is less trouble than other teaching strategies: the writing itself is instructional and really doesn't require grading.

You can use writing to encourage practice in any academic skill. I emphasize personalizing, questioning, generalizing, specifying, comparing, summarizing, and structuring. Most teaching stops at simple exposure: children hear about the ideas and are expected to remember them. These seven skills help students move from simple exposure to experience with manipulating and connecting ideas into new concepts. They lead the child to our final goal: application of the attitudes and knowledge to understanding the issues and solving the problems in their lives.

Personalizing, Connecting, and Translating

Public concepts, what is "out there" in the collective mind, must be perceived and reconceived into the student's personal thoughts. Simple exposure to raw pieces of data and definition does not forge concepts in students' minds. Laura entered ninth grade with a lot of information. She certainly had a personal idea of economy even though she did not use the word. She knew the price of dog food, the store that had Science Diet for Puppies, the importance of proper nutrition, the drain on the household income that a puppy causes, and the ideas of rich and poor, luxuries and necessities. At fourteen she started working at a grocery store; there she saw the deliveries from the distributors, the shelves of variety and exotic foods, the shifting prices, and the signs about lettuce growers' strikes. She had all the data necessary to acquire ideas of supply and demand, resources and scarcity, poverty and wealth, standard of living and social class, capitalism and socialism, developed country and less developed country, agriculture and industry, and national and international economy. Why didn't she? She never connected those "school" ideas to her "real life" experiences. If she had, she would have perceived slaughtering dogs for food differently.

Real comprehension of ideas means experience with them. The student should be able to connect them with other personal and social knowledge. If students really understand, they should be able to restate them in their own language and then explain them in someone else's.

I often start new units with *focused freewriting*. I might begin a unit on economy by saying, "For three minutes, write anything that comes into your mind about economics. The only rule is that you must write constantly from the time I say to go until the time I tell you to stop." Then I ask the students to share something from the freewriting; or I might just walk around the room and skim over some of them myself while they write. If Laura were in that class, I would know immediately the level of her understanding. She would have written, "I can't think of anything to write about economy. Is it part of government?" And so on. The student also sees what she knows and can compare her first freewriting, focused on economy, with a final freewriting which is a much fuller and more informed piece of writing about economy.

In that class, which is senior level, I might also ask students to take *personal double-entry notes.* For double-entry notes, students take traditional class notes on the left two-thirds of each page, but they leave a large right margin, maybe two inches. For economics, I ask students to take class notes, as they do, and to add relevant personal experiences next to the notes in the large right margin. For example, if the conventional notes were about recession, students might write, "My mom and grandmother were fired from the laundromat," "My neighbor across the street lost her job at Shearson Lehman when they got in trouble," or "Half the stores in the Scott's Corners Mall are closed." All the students are busily relating the classwork to their own experiences; sometimes those margins become topics for discussion, small-group activities, or longer papers.

In a different class I might have used *learning logs.* Instead of a loose-leaf notebook, I ask students to keep all their writing in a sewn book (like the marbled type) as a learning log. As with the freewriting, students can start a unit by writing everything they know about a key concept: recession, WWII, or immigration, for example; you can begin the learning log with a *What do you know about . . ."* essay. The students then can add to this answer as they go along in the unit. Students write frequently during class and at home; several times in one class you stop the class activity and say "Write down a *transla-tion* in your own language of what you just learned." At any time during the class, you can ask them to share that small piece of writing with a classmate and discuss it for two minutes. One of the best uses of learning logs is to give *individual homework.* A brief personal homework assignment for Laura might have been to list everything in the Shop Rite that could be considered a delicacy produced from animals. It would have broadened her concept of economy much more than any chapter from a textbook. It wouldn't have taken any time to correct; she, herself, would have been responsible for show-ing in her learning log what she had learned from that experience about "economy."

Questioning

Personalizing, connecting, and translating all show students how to use what they already know to comprehend better. After drawing out all the knowledge they can, they still need additional information to truly comprehend. One of my favorite writing activities is *listing questions* and answering them. After students know what they need to be able to do at the end of a unit—that is, after their "authentic assessment" has been described to them, and after their freewriting, which shows them what they already know—they can list all the questions they need to be able to answer in order to complete the final demonstration. Often I use a combination of lists and consensus groups. In pairs, students make a list of ten questions; two pairs get together and agree on the most essential ten; then four pairs; then eight; then the entire class. Each session is maybe three to five minutes. The entire process takes less than twenty minutes, yet every student has a stake in the resulting list. That list then becomes a set of questions they actually answer in their learning logs during class or at home.

Consensus groups

Generalizing

Remembering information depends on reconstructing old concepts into new ones. Students tend to focus on details rather than the key concept. They need to remind themselves constantly of the main ideas if they are going to build organized understandings. *Key Concept double-entry notes* can be used to focus on main ideas as well as on personal connections. In the right margin, students write the key concept every time they hear it. When they are taking notes, for example, on WWII, they might write "democracy," "economy," "imperialism," "industry," "disarmament," "nationalism," "neutrality," or whatever main idea we are discussing in the unit. *Underlining* is certainly not new. However, you might be surprised at how many students can't find the main idea either when its being discussed in class or when they're reading. I like to believe that I explain (when I do talk in class) in clean, orderly outlines. Every September, though, my students don't know, literally, what I'm talking about. They get the picayune details; their first notes are usually strings of data. Only after I've insisted that they underline class notes and text and after I've spent class time checking their underlining am I sure they really know what the main subject is. Many students don't hear what you say; listening for key concepts needs to be taught.

Glossing serves the same function. If they write the key idea in the margin whenever they find it, they begin to think in terms of central meaning. What is unique about using writing this way is not that students do it, but that it's an assigned activity that the teacher helps them master and that they must use later.

At the end of a unit, students can write a *key word paper,* a coherent essay using all the key words they've underlined or glossed in their books and notes. Students see their progress much better by comparing their key word paper to their original freewriting than seeing an *A* or a *D* on the paper.

Specifying

In high school we often teach at a level students cannot understand. "Evil" in my Eastern religions unit is just a word; the concept is simply too abstract for most normal seventeen-year-olds. "Life," a key concept in biology, is just as inaccessible. Students can be asked to list examples of evil at various levels of abstraction. *Reducing to lowest terms* is a writing activity that makes the concept more and more specific and concrete. Ask the students to list all the evil situations they can think of; they might list the Crusades, Nazism, and poverty. Then they list all evils in each. For Nazism, they might list the murder and torture of Jews, the break-up of families, and the invasion of Poland. From each of those they would generate a list; under Jews, they would probably list Anne Frank. Finally, many students even list personal experiences of abuse. The idea is analogous to reducing to lowest terms in mathematics: end up with the most concrete and specific examples possible. Literally hundreds of examples of evil at a concrete level are what build to a concept of evil that is without physical characteristics; hundreds of kinds of evil that are not specifically religious build a concept of evil that is connected to religion. Laura's concept of "economics" could have been improved if she had been asked to reduce "economy" to lowest terms. Ultimately, she would have gotten to Shop Rite and maybe even to goose-liver pâté and veal cutlets.

Comparison and Contrast

How are subcultures in the U. S. like the ingredients in a German chocolate cake? How is evolution like cultural development? What is *x* in the analogy "bottle:baby = *x*:justice?" In *formal analogies* like these the student uses the analogy as a topic sentence and then proves it point by point. You can do the same with *mad libs.* In their learning logs or just on a sheet of looseleaf, let the students each write a sentence ending such as ". . . is like a glowing sunset in the fall"; then you put in a key concept "democracy," or "force," and let them prove the resulting statement, no matter how silly. *Mad libs* often generate excellent connections and force students to exercise their powers of comparing.

Another good way of clarifying a concept is by contrast, identifying a set by listing nonmembers. You can use *direct contrast*. If you're discussing violence in U. S. society, stop the class and ask everyone to write a three-minute contrast of our society to a nonviolent society. Or you can ask them to write the answer to "What if . . . ?" questions. To understand the protective function of laws, ask "What if the legal drinking age were six?" A third effective strategy using contrast is *believing* and *doubting*. When the discussion is about an idea like "Steve Biko was a racist," ask students to spend four minutes writing: they have to spend two minutes believing *every* implication of a concept and justify their assertions; then they spend another two minutes doubting and explaining those doubts. When they have finished, those writings can be shared with the entire class, with a partner, or not at all. They can be used as impetus to another writing assignment.

Writing activities like these can occur at any time during a class. They can focus the discussion or spark discussion. Students can be asked to share the writings with one other classmate and write a response; or they can be asked to share a part with the entire class.

Structuring and Classifying

Main concepts can be outlined, mapped, treed, or put into word webs. Had Laura had much more experience with organizing in social studies and science, she might have automatically known what to compare; she would have known that you compare things of similar levels or logical types. Laura might have thought of her argument as a hierarchical word web (see Figure 6-2). If she mentally organized hierarchically in this way, she would have seen that what she would do with her puppies is logically irrelevant unless she deals specifically with how people in the Philippines deal with their pets; they may, so far as she knows, adore chickens. She might also see that the president of the U. S. may be as culpable as the president of the Philippines or that the president of the Philippines is no more "the people" than the president of the U.S. is "the people," i.e., Laura herself.

A *framed essay* is another form of structuring. In this case, the teacher provides the structure and part of the content before the student begins to write. A framed essay is the opposite of a word web. In a word web, the concept is first; in a framed essay the order is first and the idea fits into it. The teacher writes the topic sentences and

Figure 6-2

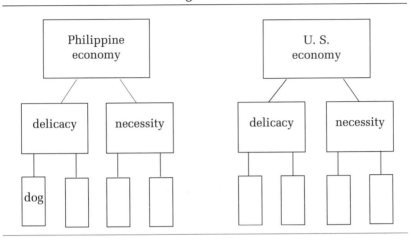

the transitions for an essay about a key concept. In some ways, a frame is a giant fill-in-the-blank intended to suggest one logic of a topic while the student is still manipulating details; it is better than short fill-in-the-blank because the student must generate the details and make their development parallel. The framed essay in Figure 6-3 was assigned to an anthropology class working on the concept of "culture." It is part of a series of framed paragraphs which lead up to a fifteen- to twenty-page essay defining "culture." The student knew from the first day of the course that she would be working toward that long piece of writing and that the frames were simply interim aids to developing her personal organization.

In this framed essay, Kimmie demonstrates knowledge, attitudes, and skills similar to Laura's. The most obvious attitude is the ethnocentrism that causes her to view her culture's rituals as "civilized" as opposed to the Kikuyu's. Just as Laura was revolted at the idea of eating dogs, Kimmie is disgusted by smoking bodies "like bacon or something"; she doesn't, in fact, deal with the idea that cremation isn't so different from smoking bodies. Nor does she consider how the Kikuyus might view our putting people (whom they treat as alive) into the ground. The last line of the frame implies a key attitude concept of the course, that Western cultures frequently call tribal cultures or ancient cultures "uncivilized" or "primitive" because they don't not understand them. She explicitly contradicts the overt "frame" statement, "Neither one is really better in itself; it's simply more appropriate to its culture" when she asserts boldly that the

Figure 6-3A

The U.S. and the ___*Ku*___ rituals are alike because

both of them preserve their dead, the Americans using embalming fluid, and the Ku's by smoking them (he bacon or something. They both mourn but the
They are also different, however, because *American way is somewhat different. more civilized.*
→ The *Ku's just put their dead on a bluff overlooking the village whereas the Americans either bury them or cremate them & stick them in an urn somewhere.*

Each of these rituals is suited to its own culture. The United States ritual is right for modern North Americans because *Americans are more civilized, and tend to be neat, efficient, quiet & respectful about subjects such as death*

The ___*Kikuyu*___ ritual is similarly suited to *Ku's They are noisy, disgusting little varmints, and if it weren't for fear of the dead person's spirit coming back & haunting them, the cowards would probably just ditch them in the woods somewhere.*
Neither one is really better in itself; it's simply more appropriate to its culture.

Kikuyus are "noisy, disgusting little varmints, and if it weren't for fear of the dead persons's spirit coming back and haunting them, the cowards would probably just ditch them in the woods somewhere."

Yet there are two major differences between Kimmie and Laura. First, Kimmie was in the first quarter of her tenth grade year when she wrote this framed essay. Second, she had at least three classes that emphasized academic thinking between this essay and graduation. These classes focused explicitly on developing academic

Figure 6-3B

In the United States today, we have marriage, puberty, and death rituals also. For example, getting and driving a car is a kind of modern puberty ritual for boys. Choose either marriage, puberty, or death rituals and show how our ritual is the same, and different from the ritual of one of the tribes we studied.

You should write your answer within this frame. I have given you the overall shape and the transitions. You may change the frame if you want, but discuss the reasons for your changes with me before you hand in your work.

Our _death_ (marriage, puberty, or _death_) rituals in the U.S. are both like and unlike the _death_ rituals of the _Kikuyu_ (tribe you've chosen). People in the United States _bury their dead, mourn them quietly, have viewings at funeral homes, and are really quite civilized about the whole thing._ The _Ku's_ (your tribe), on the other hand,

tear their hair, smear themselves with dirt, throw themselves on the ground & beat themselves bloody, don't bury their dead & treat the bodies like they were still alive even going so far as to put food in their mouths.

---

attitudes, skills, and knowledge; all three used frequent "authentic assessments." Through framed essays, word webs, and group activities, she began to internalize the formal logic of this kind of academic argument.

I never had to have a conference with Kimmie like the ones I had with Laura; her classmates did it when they shared their framed essays and tried to develop a group framed essay. They, of course, confronted her directly, "How do you know that Kikuyu teenagers wouldn't think is was revolting that you'd dump their little old grandmother in a hole the ground? I think it's a little disgusting myself now that I think of it!" "I wouldn't want my sister smoked, but I wouldn't want her burned to ashes and stuck in an urn either!" "You think some of the stuff we do is civilized? I think standing around like you're having a cocktail party when someone you love is dead is uncivilized. When my friend died it wouldn't have been so bad if I could have thrown myself on the ground and screamed." By the end of the year, Kimmie began to show the detachment necessary to put herself in the place of the Kikuyus and other peoples.

Both hierarchical word webs and framed paragraphs are highly analytic, "Western" academic structures. They are used only as methods of teaching a particular academic way of organizing. Students need to know that there are other choices, but that this kind of strict hierarchical understanding is one of the skills that an academic thinker must be able to use.

Grading Writing

Double entry notes, freewriting, learning logs, key-word papers, word webs, and framed essays are not final compositions for grading any more than small group activities are final products for grading. These pieces of writing are "epistemic," that is, writing to learn. They're used in social studies, science, and sometimes mathematics, as well as in English. They should be graded as "done" or "not done," "+" or "0," "pass" or "fail." They should not be evaluated for quality of ideas or writing proficiency. Kimmie's framed essay, for example, while it had some glaring inadequacies as a piece of writing, fulfilled the assignment. The grade was a "pass." The revisions necessary in thoughts and writing came from subsequent class processes, not the grade. The teacher schedules activities that allow the student to see what she has been thinking, to revise her thoughts, and to develop her academic skills and knowledge.

Changing Students: A Conclusion

All of these learning strategies are simply structured forms of intellectual processing which most "academic" thinkers employ habitually and unconsciously: *personalizing* (double-entry notes, freewriting, learning logs), *generalizing* (double-entry notes, learning logs) *comparing* and *contrasting* (analogies, *mad libs,* speculating and questioning, believing and doubting), and *structuring* and *classifying* (outlining, webbing, and framing). Any other class activities that have the same effect are as valuable.

The purpose is to get students from here to there. When Laura reads the *Star* again someday, we wish she could think of parallel governments. When she votes, we want her to pull the lever for the person who best serves the country rather than the candidate who exploits her powerful feelings for animals.

Therefore, none of these methods should be used as one-shot gimmicks. They're external modes of helping childen develop internal resources. If you tell students to keep double-entry notes and use the right margin to make personal connections, you should assign that strategy for an entire semester. The point is to have students begin thinking in terms of personal connections. At the end of a semester, you want to have altered their thinking patterns.

These methods also alter study and learning skills: reading, writing, listening, speaking, and notetaking. Glossing and underlining, for example, make reading and listening much more academic. All of the activities give students more options in writing as well as thinking.

Just as students must be told explicitly what attitudes and knowledge will accomplish their goals, they must also be made aware of the reasons they are practicing skills. Double-entry notetaking looks fairly stupid to a child who has no idea he might be acquiring the ability to identify and develop his thoughts this way or that developing those thoughts benefit him.

Most teachers don't attempt to teach thinking explicitly at all. We assume that a student's ability to acquire and use knowledge is already determined by socioeconomic and physiological characteristics. Therefore, feeling helpless to change the child's ability to learn, we try to change everything else. We test, label, and track. Not too long ago, I was a consultant in a district that actually had five different tracks from the lowest track, actually called "00"s, to the highest, called "honors". Once we classify students by their "ability," then we provide appropriate environments, curriculum, or methods: programmed texts, contained classrooms, open classrooms, team teaching, flexible schedules, electives, and audio/visual aids. If none of those work, then there is the psychologist, the residential school, or maybe even the jail.

If we want children to think and learn academically, we must teach them academic thinking. There's certainly evidence that thinking can be taught, that "ability" can be changed. There's the evidence of research and there's the evidence of all the Lauras and Kimmies we have seen in our classes. We all learn to think. Every morning some kid in the "00" class gets up, walks out the door, and takes her bus to school. She thinks every second of the trip; she doesn't deal with every single item she encounters—all the blades of grass, the nine different school buses, the question of when to cross the street or indeed what a street is. Efficiently, she identifies, classifies, organizes, and stores information and moves on through the day. The difference between her and the honors student next door is not that she doesn't think but that she can't choose from a variety of patterns of thinking.

If a student does not learn academic thinking at home or at school, she won't learn academic subjects. Like most children, Laura was *taught* at one point or another everything she needed to know. Whether she *learned* depended on the method. All normal children *can* learn academic thinking—some at home; some at school; some quickly; some slowly. But no one should have to leave high school as a "00."

Chapter Seven

The Great Roe
Testing to Change Children

*The Great Roe is a mythological beast with the head of a
lion and the body of a lion, though not the same lion.*
Woody Allen

Our current testing methods carry the pernicious message that recall
of knowledge is education. Conventional tests emphasize identifying, defining, and repeating. Multiple choice, true/false, fill-in-the-
blank, and even many essays primarily test short-term memory.

Memory is certainly important. After a biology course, a student
should remember many facts, examples, and theories. How, otherwise, could adults even begin to understand a headline like "Defec-
tive Chromosome May Cause Violent Behavior"? But remembering is
just the beginning. When I read about chromosomes in the paper, I
also should be able to connect and reformulate ideas, reorganize
feelings, form opinions, and maybe even take some action. I may not
want to think about every headline academically, but I want the
power to choose. Maybe I have a violent child. Maybe, just as Laura
needed to influence the treatment of dogs, I need to have impact on
the treatment of violent behavior. No reputable teacher or district or
state really aspires to teach the lesson that information alone magi-
cally coalesces into education.

To prepare students for the future, we must also test excellence, certainty, and pleasure in *using* academic knowledge effectively. After all, in the adult world of work and family and community, people are judged, not just for their memories, but also for their decisions and actions, their projects and products, their ideals and impact. Our current tests mostly ask students to remember what other people have done. Direct assessments also demonstrate the student's ability to "do."

"Direct" assessment means directly testing what we want students to be able to do when they finish a lesson, a unit, a course, or their secondary education. It's also sometimes called "authentic," "performance," or "appropriate" assessment. Alternative schools like St. Paul Open School in Minnesota and Mountain Open School in Colorado have used direct assessments for as long as I've been teaching. Many conventional disciplines assess students' accomplishment directly: foreign languages assess speaking, reading, comprehending and writing; music has recitals; and the arts have portfolios and exhibits. Many states assess writing by asking students to write. The goals of those disciplines are reflected in the assessments. We study language to speak, listen, write, and read. We study music and art to understand and produce music and art. Why do we study literature, history, and biology?

After we leave high school, we must be able to talk and write; to form and express opinions; to take informed action; to enjoy and produce art, music, and literature; to help ourselves and others; to do our jobs; and to augment our freedom, power, health, and happiness. If we want Don to be able to vote analytically and thoughtfully, his test should require him to gather, classify, and analyze information, to choose a candidate, and to explain his choice. Why, instead, do we usually ask him multiple choice questions on the history of political parties? How many multiple choice questions will he have to answer after he graduates?

Right now, we ask recall questions most of the time. In high school, our adolescents study slavery, the Civil War, and the civil rights movement in U. S. History; Nelson Mandela in global studies; *Plessy vs. Ferguson* in government; and *Huckleberry Finn* in U. S. literature. If they remember those studies at all, they seldom remember them past the end of the marking period. They don't necessarily connect the experiences with their lives, and they probably won't use them to form opinions, make decisions, or take actions. These students aren't changed by our classes. If they are not capable of being more informed about diverse cultures, more tolerant and empathetic, more skilled in dealing with one another, then we, and schooling, have failed.

Being required to *use* knowledge and skills moves children well beyond the level of most current tests. We don't, in fact, have to give up all conventional testing. The first stage of learning in a classroom is ordinarily the exposure level; the first stage of assessment can be at the same level. The teacher introduces material and the child understands well enough to identify, remember, and repeat it. Exposure is the level of most multiple choice, fill-in-the-blank, and true-false tests. Occasionally those tests may be useful, if limited.

Even at this level, however, we have to be careful. Some secondary school students aren't ready for multiple choice, true/false, and fill-in-the-blank. Those tests can actually discriminate against the "ordinary person" who has no experience in academic thinking. While they ostensibly require memory, they actually require general knowledge, academic skills, and positive attitudes toward learning; they also rest on considerable self-esteem, confidence, and persistence. If, on a biology test, students have to match the word "chromosome" to a definition and they can't, maybe they aren't just lazy. Maybe we have to help them, even at this early level, by using small groups and epistemic writing.

Usually, even at the exposure level, there are better ways to assess recognition and recall anyway. The purpose of quizzes is to help teachers decide how and what to teach and to show students what they've learned. Teachers can easily observe students, read their informal writings, and confer with them more often instead of relying almost exclusively on traditional tests. Almost any activity, if the student is really "active," can be a "test" as well as a learning experience. Assessment can occur any time and any place. Even small quizzes are best when they directly assess what we really want students to be able to do. Why are vocabulary quizzes always "matching" or "definitions"? Ultimately students use words to talk, write and read. If you introduce words on Monday, students can be expected to use the words before the next Monday. Whenever a student uses a word properly (you tell her if she doesn't), she writes the date and the word on a notecard and drops the card in a box on your desk. At the end of the week, you check off how many she's used. That method is less trouble than a written quiz; and it's a better test. It tests pronunciation and use as well as recall. It also encourages students to experiment with new words and to play with meanings. When Damon, one of my tenth-grade students, didn't use any words one week, he came to me, and, with a burlesque shrug of his shoulders, said, "I'm omni-sorry!"

The same kind of direct assessment works for major concepts in literature, history, or science. In English, for example, there really needn't be a test in which children define metaphor and identify one in a poem. In adulthood, metaphorical language enriches our lives day by day, not on tests. During a poetry unit, the class might be discussing Ruth Whitman's poem "The Castoff Skin." As small groups discuss the poem, the teacher records who understands the snake metaphor. When the students write their own poetry, she notes who uses a metaphor. Why should we continue to use tests, even little ones, that work against education?

At the next level, the experience or comprehension level, the students should be able not only to connect the information or skill to previous knowledge but also restructure it in their own minds. We can, and sometimes do, assess the comprehension level by essay tests. If we want to teach children organizing, connecting, and speculating, we have to ask them to use these academic skills. Even so, quite honestly, most of our essays are just fill-in-the-*big*-blank. The questions are predictable. Almost always the right answer is laid out in class. The students only have to know the formula for an "expository essay" and be able to fill in the blanks with the information taught. Even our essay tests often focus on fragmented facts, not integrated concepts, and on memory itself, not use of information. Right now, we test a lot of data and very little thought.

Finally, in the highest stage of academic thinking, students should be able to use skills and knowledge confidently and automatically to reflect on an issue, to complete a task, or to solve a problem. If we want confidence, persistence, or pleasure, we must test those attitudes. If we want students to be able to use history to make decisions or use biology to solve problems, then we must make them demonstrate that they can. In the real world, no discipline exists alone. So, while authentic tasks involve control over the specific "know-how" and "know-what" of each discipline, they also involve general thinking skills like reading, writing, speaking, listening, calculating, analyzing, synthesizing, patterning, predicting, and judging. Testing at the level of application can assess integration of information, higher order thinking skills, and appropriate attitudes. The application level is actually well beyond the achievement now required by most local and state tests. It is, however, one level of effective adulthood.

Changing our tests changes us and, ultimately, changes our students. Everyone teaches "to the test." What if Laura's teachers, from kindergarten on, had had as one of their goals: Laura must be able to use social studies concepts to take action on public issues. Then, way back in first and second grade, they would have known that she needed certain values, skills, and information. Sure, some of her learning would have been the same; it would have involved memory, comprehension, and application of traditional disciplines. After all, these "academics" are profound visions and powerful tools. Physics, for example, has evolved for hundreds of years. The accumulated wisdom of Pascal, Copernicus, Newton, and Einstein, however, is only valuable for Laura in her own mind. Her teachers would have focused all along on how Laura's mind had to change in order to use those disciplines to accomplish her own goals. Then, when her real world test came up, she would have been able to think critically and write persuasively about the Philippines. Focusing on students' individual minds rather than materials to cover, makes teaching simpler.

When teachers can define accomplishment partly by what students can do, we can resolve many long-standing curricular problems. The teacher's job is to identify important concepts and skills and teach children to use them; teachers must work toward student performance rather than focus on the textbook. What students don't know becomes insignificant; what they can know, cherish, and use is vital. In that perspective, debates about "cultural literacy" or "the curriculum of inclusion," for example, become much easier to resolve.

What a lot of time we've spent debating what constitutes "cultural literacy" (Hirsch 1988). Of course, one of our goals is to create and perpetuate a common heritage and shared values. However, even though there are key ideas that most citizens should share, effective adulthood doesn't require one right set of specific information. In fact, if we succeeded in teaching every single student just "what every seventeen year old" *should* know, (Ravitch 1988), we would create a remarkably uniform and sterile community. On the other hand, if we had a set of tasks that every seventeen year old could perform, then students could share values, skills, and knowledge productively.

The fierce debate about "multicultural education" or "the curriculum of inclusion" also becomes less heated when we stop trying to solve it solely by choosing information fairly. Practically every state social studies syllabus already lists goals such as "increasing students' awareness of ethnic diversity" and "encouraging students' personal and cultural self-esteem." Those are attitudes. You don't change attitudes simply by including particular information in the syllabus. Black children in New York City have a history, hundreds of years, of slavery and oppression. Their cultural heritage includes the economic and family suffering described by Mary Berry and John Blassingame in *Long Memory* (1982). A black child does not become proud just because Martin Luther King is included in his social studies book. It's useless to argue about what percentage of Black, Japanese, or Latino history will make our children proud or tolerant.

When teachers actually have to teach to a direct demonstration of pride, they have to put down the textbook and work to identify what will really help each individual child acquire it. Exactly how effective is information in changing deeply felt attitudes? How much does working collaboratively with students of other races and ethnic groups in the classroom influence attitudes? How important are models? People seem to become less prejudiced and more empathetic when they learn about diverse cultures. They seem to become less ethnocentric and can see stereotypes and biases when they learn "scientific reasoning." How important are these skills in reducing racism? Pride can't be measured on a multiple choice test; it can't be taught from a textbook. If my job is teaching children pride in their cultural heritage, I am successful only when those children demonstrate their pride directly.

Teaching itself is also simpler when all students are expected to achieve high standards of effective adulthood. If, as teachers, we think systematically about what our students will be to be able to do after graduation, we'll also think of our job as teaching future neighbors. Then we see graduates as we see auto mechanics, surgeons, and musicians: we don't want to experience, personally, the results of sixty-five percent achievement. However, we can still take account of their different learning and doing styles as well as their diverse backgrounds, interests, and goals. Since there are many right answers, students can acquire information, make decisions, and solve problems in a variety of ways. We work more effectively so that all students *can* achieve high standards.

Students work harder because they know what they have to be able to do and the standards of excellence in doing it. Activities, like visiting a museum, reading the textbook, or drawing a map, are related directly to a particular important adult task. Students can see that through the academic disciplines, they are acquiring the power to comprehend, reflect, predict, and act in the adult world of choices and consequences.

In the real world, no one looks for answers unless she has questions. Often teachers try to motivate students with provocative questions: "Are you for or against the death penalty?" But then the same teachers allow the sloppiest answers. Students parrot their parents and their friends. They argue by repeating themselves and picking holes in the other students' logic or by resorting to pathos and personal stories. Why not? They're using common sense, the only method many of them know. We shouldn't let them.

Death, life, friendship, marriage, religion, and environment are all essential issues for adults to confront. Why not use those questions about the death penalty to directly test their understanding and use of global studies or literature? If you start with a real issue, someone from your town who is scheduled to be executed, you could then let them write to the governor using cross-cultural and historical, literary, or biological information to prove their opinions. An assignment like that doesn't take a week, though. In a month, you might be able to give them enough help that they could actually use different world views, different attitudes toward life, death, individuality, society, and crime to discover and clarify the issues. That's one way students can learn disciplined, academic thought. School should help answer the question "What kind of adult do I choose to be?" That's genuine motivation, finding knowledge and skills that solve profound problems.

The "coverage" way emphasizes someone else's answer to a question you never asked; it trivializes school and makes learning memorization. Direct assessment, on the other hand, emphasizes providing questions, not answers. The textbook is the resource not the focus. The student sees information as a tool to help decide and act. Direct assessments help students do what adults do. All students have the right to be able to be effective adults: citizens, parents, children, consumers, producers, neighbors, and individuals. Our tests determine what kind of adults our students can choose to be.

Developing direct assessments is easy. The first step is to ask, "What do I want students to be able to do after they finish my course?" For global studies, a ninth and tenth grade sequence, I've decided that the overall goal is to help students be capable of skilled, informed, active, and committed world citizenship; world citizens should be able to:

1. identify important global, national, state, or local issues

2. make ethical and practical decisions about these issues by identifying a variety of choices, speculating about and evaluating consequences of alternative methods, choosing appropriate actions, and carrying through with the actions

3. solve personal and social problems

4. identify, clarify, express, and act on feelings and goals

The students must use the major concepts, attitudes and skills of world history, world geography and sociology to accomplish these central acts of adulthood.

I like portfolios as the overall, final assessment to show how students achieved these goals. A portfolio is a collection of the students' writings, videotapes, audiotapes, and illustrations comparable to an art portfolio. All portfolios are different, of course; they vary according to the school, the year, the teacher, and the students. However, mine always have five parts: introduction, goals, required demonstrations, optional demonstrations, and evaluations.

The introduction to the portfolio specifies the students' own ideas about what they can demonstrate in a portfolio. Jennifer, one of my students, writes in her introduction:

> . . . The RCT [Regents' Competency Test in New York] has been designed by the state to see what the students of New York have learned. . . . In other words, by the state for the state. My portfolio was by me, for me, and for the state. The RCT doesn't show the state what I have learned. It only shows them that I studied for their test. . . . In my portfolio, I will not only be stating dates and events, I will be expressing personal feelings and my reactions towards national, international, and day to day events. . . . Everything inside this portfolio is my work, not like on the RCT where you just see my pencil marks. As an individual I can show my creativity and my growth a a person as well as my growth as a student. The RCT does not offer me that. The RCT also doesn't show the progress a student makes in a year. As you look through and read my portfolio, you will see the tremendous change in my writing, thinking and expressing skills. What do colored-in dots on an answer sheet show you?

The second major section, goals, begins with two pieces of writing, the students' personal goals for global studies and their speculations about the overall value of history and sociology. The personal goals always relate to the students' unique needs, their families, their dreams, and their fears. Jen's center on her need to be in control of her life. The uses-of-history essay is more general. History, Jen says,

> is the axis on which this planet spins. Some people look at history as a bunch of useless dates and boring, old stories. If you're smart, you know this statement is not true. Everything that the past holds is a key to our future. Without the knowledge of old wars and the decisions that the great leaders of the past made, our decisions today would be a lot harder and riskier to make.

Then she goes on to say how studying Hitler, Roosevelt, and other historical figures can influence her decisions. As Jen continues in the course, her personal goals and ideas about history may change. When she rewrites, however, she'll include all of her early versions.

In the third section, "Required Demonstrations," students include writing, audiotapes and videotapes, and illustrations that demonstrate how they've met their goals. For the teacher, there are two steps in designing demonstrations: choosing a subject and choosing a form. In global studies, I organize around geography just as the state syllabus does. In a half-year, we might study Africa, the Middle East, and the former Soviet Union and Eastern Europe. The activity is one or more of these four central acts of adulthood: identifying issues, clarifying feelings, making decisions, and solving problems.

One way to choose the particular "ethical and practical decisions" or the "personal and immediate social problems" is by an old-fashioned current events class once a week. Students choose articles and share them in class during current events. From these discussions come some of the main demonstration topics for the next units. The year the government of South Africa finally moved to end apartheid, for example, one of our topics was "Would you be more likely to buy from a company with investments in South Africa now than you would have ten years ago?" Issues don't have to come from current events, of course. Sometimes they might be economic or moral decisions which interest students or they could be questions taken from texts like *Reasoning with Democratic Values* (Lockwood and Harris 1985).

By the end of the unit, students must demonstrate that they can use knowledge, skills, and attitudes to deal with these issues. The form of demonstrations is usually an activity that adults actually perform; thinking, talking, writing, and doing. Round table discussions demonstrate educated conversation. Formal presentations to other students, parents, and community members demonstrate teaching, parenting, and group leadership. We also use letters actually mailed to individuals, and we use poetry, stories, and essays submitted to the public press.

Part of designing the demonstration is setting standards of excellence. For every unit, the students need to know what a good performance is as well as what they must be able to do. For each kind of demonstration, we find examples of excellence. If we are writing letters, we read famous letters. If we are doing a community project, we look at similar adult projects that worked well. Whatever the overall activity, students know they will be judged holistically against these exemplars. There are only two possible grades for credit, "good" and "excellent." Students must continue working until they achieve those standards.

In Jen's class, we did three unit demonstrations in one semester. We started studying Africa in December. In that unit, the students' goal was informed participation in a round table discussion, four students and two outside experts, about whether each student should buy UNICEF cards. To establish standards, we asked "How do effective adults use history and sociology to make decisions? How do they discuss those issues?" That year we were lucky; it was easy to find examples. We could watch Congressional debates about sending troops to Kuwait; we heard the senators and the President using history to make that decision. We watched "Meet the Press" and "Face the Nation" also.

In some people's ordinary lives, the answer to the UNICEF card question could be "No, why should I get up Saturday morning to buy expensive cards when I can get them at Caldor's cheaper and easier?" We all decide that way sometimes; we couldn't live in the world if every small decision required ethical agony. In a global studies class, though, students should be learning the attitude that we can make reasoned decisions about our actions, even small ones. Information helps us make choices, solve problems, live by our values, and delight in ideas. We are also explicitly teaching students that they are capable of, and responsible for, influencing their world, not just by voting, but also by everyday shopping, raising children, and going to the movies. So a simple "No, I could care less" is very far from "good" or "excellent."

We studied the areas of Africa where UNICEF was active; we also investigated the history of charity, the United Nations and UNICEF, and the students' own values. All of the students read parts of a quite traditional textbook about Africa. Most of them visited the UN and UNICEF. They all also had to answer the questions, "What is your role in your community? Should you help others?" "What does 'your community,' involve? Just your town? The entire world?" Naturally, they also had to be prepared, articulate, and persuasive. So most of them practiced their discussions with peer groups.

Besides the assignments everyone did, individuals did special reading and writing, went to the African museum, visited consulates, and ate at an Ethiopian restaurant. A student from an Albanian family analyzed the Albanian world view to show why he would not buy the cards. Another student showed why he thought environmental waste was more detrimental to life than starvation in Africa.

After three weeks of preparation, students finally demonstrated that they could use history, culture, and geography to make informed ethical decisions. Each student's preparation and discussion was unique. As in our adult world, there are various ways to achieve excellence.

When Jennifer's class studied the Middle East, during Iraq's invasion of Kuwait and the subsequent war between Iraq and the United Nations' forces, the students wrote letters to their own unborn children about how their lives were affected by the war; the letters were to be saved and actually given to their children in twenty-five years. They also wrote and published relevant poetry. Again, to write the letters and poetry, they had to understand the history, politics, and religion of the Middle East. In these demonstrations, however, the emphasis was on understanding, expressing, and communicating feelings and beliefs in the context of other value systems.

Jen's class studied what was then the Soviet Union and Eastern Europe in the spring. We had a guest speaker who brought along thirteen Afghani orphans flown to the United States for medical help. Our project was to write letters to the Islamic Cultural Center about ways we would like to help deal with those and similar children. Jennifer's letter had to take account of the history and culture of those children as well as the current political situation in Afghanistan. The purpose of the final letter was to demonstrate the students' abilities to empathize with people far away, to understand complex political situations, and to begin to solve, in quite personal ways, international problems.

The portfolio entries for "Required Demonstrations" were the videotapes of the roundtable discussions, letters to their unborn children and the Islamic Cultural Center, and poetry. Students also included the diagrams, graphs, maps, drafts, outlines, trip journals, and notes done in preparation.

In the "Optional Demonstrations" section of the portfolio, many of the students included their relevant personal poetry and fiction. They also entered a current events journal based on our regular current events class. One of the course goals, after all, was: "identify important global, national, state, or local issues." Just as with other demonstrations, we established standards for current events. Throughout the year, if students chose articles capriciously, read carelessly, presented inexpertly, connected or evaluated poorly, I conferred with them. Even in this small current events activity, students were expected, and helped, to be "good" or "excellent."

There's nothing sacred about round table discussions or letters as unit assessments. The form of the assessment, whether it's equivalent to a quiz, a unit test, or a final exam, grows from the goals of the discipline. One goal of chemistry and physics is to help students understand and manipulate ideas dispassionately; so a round table discussion, which involves a great deal of interpretation, analogizing, and speculating, may not be appropriate at all. Advanced physics is more related to philosophy than history; the point is to formulate generalizable models that transcend individual differences; so another goal is that students find satisfaction in the precision, regularity, and predictability of these models. That goal is close to learning for learning's sake. In physics, an opinion letter to a service organization might be totally inappropriate. We don't want to teach that the main purpose of learning science is application; we don't want to reduce advanced physics to the physics of everyday phenomena. In physics and chemistry, some of our end products should involve dispassionate, precise, and orderly manipulation of the data.

At the end of each year in global studies, after putting all their required and optional demonstrations into the portfolio, students wrote self-evaluations to put in the "Evaluation" section of their portfolios. I also entered a narrative description of each student's progress. At the end of the two-year course sequence, an outside evaluator assessed the entire portfolio. Outside evaluators for the portfolio and the individual units assess students' performance holistically on a six-point scale (see Appendix). Of course, there are a variety of other scoring methods. Most of them, however, can be translated into numbers to be used on a class, district, state, or national level. They are, naturally, "criterion referenced" not "norm referenced."

When I look at Jennifer's completed portfolio, I can see Jennifer, what she believes, what she loves, what she can do. Jen started the course when she was fourteen; she completed it at sixteen. I certainly see progress in her writing, her skills, and her attitudes; I also see exactly what she knows and how she uses that information. But her character and style stand out: she's fascinated with color and design. All her outlines are color coded, and her title pages created on the computer are decorated in bold colors. Her portfolio is quite different from Beth's, which is hand bound in tapestry and illustrated in Beth's own fragile watercolors. On Jennifer's audiotapes, I hear her weave her personal stories into our common history. On her videotapes, I see her passion to improve the world in the way she leans forward. When she talks, she speaks about her family heritage of social action. I can watch her struggle with the course goals and slowly recognize the meaning of poverty in Africa: "For fourteen cents," she says on one videotape, "I can save a child from dehydration. I have fourteen cents everywhere . . . under the seat of my car." At the same time I see her increasing skill at using facts, charts, graphs and maps to develop and document her opinions. Reading through her portfolio is, as Jennifer says herself in her introduction, "the most exciting ride of your life, a ride through the mind of a student." The portfolio demonstrates what Jennifer is and can be.

I use portfolios to send to the state as a final state evaluation of the two-year global studies sequence and also of the one-year U. S. history course. I could have chosen any number of other forms for the final assessment: evidence (or "research") papers, interviews, performances, or community projects. The portfolio or these other direct assessments can demonstrate a student's expertise in high school literature, mathematics, sociology, history, physics, chemistry, biology, or earth science, as well as social studies.

For most children, "academic" wisdom is learned in school. Direct assessments make us think about what we want the children to be and to do; they demonstrate clearly whether our students have the skills and knowledge they need. Direct assessments give Don the opportunity to begin school Don and end school Don, but *not* the same Don. The new Don is able to use academic patterns of mind to accomplish the tasks of adulthood.

Chapter Eight

From Here To There
A Unit Using Direct Assessment, Epistemic Writing, and Small Groups

By the time I retire, I will have taught more than 3000 students. My husband and many of my friends are also teachers. Six or seven of us have taught probably 20,000 people.

If even a third of those people have made it "there"—have more power to consider, judge, choose, and act, are more skilled, knowledgeable, committed, and active, have healthier, more satisfied and productive lives—my half-dozen friends and I have changed our world.

One teacher can make a difference. Seven teachers can make a big difference. But when I look back at my teaching, I don't think of the thousands of students my colleagues and I *might* have changed significantly. I see the individual faces of students who, I know, changed profoundly. I see Becky.

Becky entered my class in the second quarter of ninth grade. Her academic record was terrible; she'd spent more than half of sixth, seventh, and eighth grades out of school. The day she arrived, I started a unit on the Arabian Gulf. Becky sat down toward the back of the room and received this assignment:

> By 12/20, you will be able to answer the question: Would you buy *The Satanic Verses* if you were living in New York City? Teheran? To answer this question you will need to know:
> 1. The world view, religion, culture, geography and politics of the Middle East
> 2. Your own culture's world view and your personal values

On 12/20 or 12/21, you will discuss the question with a community expert and four other students. On those two days, you may only bring into class three or fewer 4 x 6 notecards.
On 12/22, you must turn in a completed study book.

Who knows what Becky thought about the assignment. She didn't say anything; she looked small and bewildered. Obviously, *The Satanic Verses* isn't the real question; the main point isn't about buying a particular book written by an Indian novelist. Rushdie's book was in the news. People who went into real bookstores in New York City and London felt intimidated. The newspapers were full of terrorist threats against Salman Rushdie's life. The point is that adults should be able to make reasoned decisions about their actions.

Some of the others, though, less shy, articulated thoughts Becky might not even have dared to think: "What? I wouldn't want to buy it anyway. Who reads?" "What do I care?" "I can buy any book I want." "I wouldn't spend $19.95 for a book if it was the story of my own life."

Class Period 1

Immediately after I explained the assignment, my students began working in six groups of five. In these groups they read selections from *The Satanic Verses* and news articles about the Ayatollah Khomeini's *fatwa*. Then they spent five minutes writing questions. I walked around occasionally commenting, "scaffolding," to help them develop the questions. I carried a small steno pad with a couple of pages for each student so I could make brief notes about their questioning and interacting skills; I added Becky's two pages. For the whole of that first semester, I systematically mentioned their skills to a couple of students each day, usually as they left the class. Mostly I made observations like, "I notice that you helped the group stay on task" or "You seemed to have trouble keeping your attention on the task." Sometimes these comments resulted in a one- or two-minute individual conference, but an equally important result was that the groups started picking up my language and the class goals—"on task," "prepared," "focused," and "cooperative," for example.

Then each group reported its questions to the rest of the class while the class secretary, a student who had been chosen by the others earlier in the year, wrote the questions on an easel: "Would someone want to write a book enough to die?" "Would someone want to publish it enough?" "Would you want your father to have written a book you might die for?" "Who gave a foreign religious leader, writing in a foreign language, the right to condemn the author and publishers to death?"

In the third major part of the class, we all wrote for three uninterrupted minutes everything that came into our heads about the situation. Six students volunteered to share their freewriting. After each one read, the class clapped. The sharing brought together new and old information. It also showed Becky that thinking aloud and taking risks were admirable.

Obviously, my emphasis in this class was questioning. Students had to develop their questioning skills if they were ever to understand from an allocentric perspective. Allocentrism, seeing all or many points of view, is one of the course attitude goals. Throughout the class, I did no "traditional" teaching.

Finally, in the last couple of minutes, I congratulated them on their good beginning. Then I directed their attention to the list of reading and interviewing assignments for the unit, written on the easel. I also reminded them that from then on, they should watch the easel. Instructions for the day would be there as they entered and assignments for the next day would be displayed at the end of the period.

During the unit, this easel became a focal point of the classroom rather than the teacher. Everything written on the easel was eventually hung in the classroom. The assignment list as well as the question list from Period 1, for example, were posted by the next day. As students came for the next three weeks, they occasionally would write an announcement to their group or the entire class below the "Instructions for the Day." Once or twice, someone went up and wrote a joke for the day. Frequently, if they got there a little early, students would decorate the instructions tastefully.

Period 2

"How do you change the world?" was the topic for the second day. We spent about five minutes going around the room to let each student make one statement about changing the world. Students mentioned not buying cosmetics if they were developed through experiments on rabbits and not using Styrofoam; apparently those issues had come up the week before in science. Others mentioned topics from earlier global studies units, apartheid, for example. They brought up examples from the newspaper and their personal experiences.

Then students rejoined the original small groups for ten minutes to list ten seemingly insignificant acts that would have significant impact on the environment or on society. They read their lists aloud for the class secretary to record on the easel.

Each student then chose three from the list of about twenty and wrote an answer to questions like "Are wearing lipstick, drinking soda, or buying tabloids ethical acts?" More students shared this time, about half the class. Again, everyone clapped after each sharing.

I was handing out academic propaganda in this second period. Essentially, I was implying that everything you do has implications for someone, your choices are often political and ethical ones, whether you think about it or not. Responsibility is another one of the academic values that the global studies curriculm includes: world citizens should think that they are capable of influencing their world, by voting, buying, talking, writing, and doing. Some of the students objected to that opinion in their small groups and in their writing; for many of them it was a new idea.

Period 3

The third period looked quite traditional at first. I lectured about free speech, fundamentalism, immigration, and theocracies. When the students took notes, they annotated the right two-inch margin with information from the chapter on Arab immigration in Western Europe, assigned for the night before. Every fifteen minutes, I stopped long enough for students to catch up with their annotations. (I wanted students to practice connecting ideas from different sources.) During that break, I showed Becky what to do.

Period 4

Students read a chapter in class about governments in the Middle East and responded to "How do you think the history of the Middle East has influenced the Ayatollah's behavior?" As they worked, I could walk around checking the study books, marking the first few assignments "+" or "0" and checking carefully the reading and writing assignment they had done the night before about the relation of geography, politics, and military policy. Since that homework and the class work were similar, I could easily tell who needed help from skimming the homework. I needed to spend as much as five minutes with some students and less than a minute with others. I asked Becky and two others to leave their notebooks and pick them up after school so I could write more extensive notes to them during my free period.

The study notebooks were essential in this class. The students had to keep all their freewriting, lists, notes, personal writings, and other work in this sewn notebook. They were required to bring the study notebooks to class every day and take them home every night. I did almost all of my grading in class, when they were reading or working in groups. I only read three students' notebooks carefully; they were all having trouble with the work. I maintained a regular dialogue with them. For the others, I skimmed the notebooks well enough to make sure the work was done; their own writing and group work was enough instruction.

Period 5

Students worked in consensus groups all period. First, each person listed ten questions he needed to answer before he could understand the Ayatollah's behavior; the questions were to reflect what he'd learned in the readings and lectures in geography, government, economics, and religion so far. Then, using the individual members' lists, each small group had to agree on the ten most important questions. The small groups shared their questions and wrote them on the easel paper with the group leader's name after each question. As a big group, the students voted on the fifteen most important questions:

1. Did the Ayatollah actually read the *The Satanic Verses?* How much could he read from an unbiased perspective? (Tarra)

2. How does *The Satanic Verses* describe the Muslim leader? directly? by inference? (Jen)

3. Why is the punishment death? Is that related more to how dangerous Rushdie is or the Ayatollah's political needs? Is it just to dramatize the Ayatollah's political power? religious power? What is his political or religious power? (Carl)

4. Why punish the publishers if the *Qur'an* says to let God take care of disbelievers? Is the Ayatollah just making an example? (Timmy)

5. What economic effect could the death sentence have on other countries in the Middle East? (Jen)

6. How are non-Muslims treated in Iran? (Carl) How are Jews and Christians treated? How would I be treated? (Scott)

7. What *sacred* beliefs are actually being *profaned?* (Carl—p.s. Please notice our two new words in that sentence!!!!!)

8. Is wearing short skirts and smoking cigarettes a religious taboo or a social one? (Jen)

9. If the book questions about Islam, is *that* what is "profane" about it? (Jen)

10. What are the exact principles of Islam being violated besides questioning whether Mohammed was inspired by the devil? Is it religious blasphemy or is it that Rushdie is asking any kind of questions? Does the Ayatollah just feel so threatened that whenever any part of his "theocracy" is questioned he says it's blasphemy? (Timmy)

11. Why did Rushdie write the book? Is he concerned with free speech? his own religious beliefs? just showing off? (Bobby)

12. How can the Ayatollah justify murder? Is that part of his religious belief? In Islam is it right to have "holy wars"? Is that why there are terrorists in the Mideast? (Timmy)

13. How does the new Ayatollah feel? (Bobby)

14. Why did the Ayatollah have to offer money if all the Muslims all over the world are really willing to kill him because of his blasphemy? How do all the Muslims really feel? He must know people in London. How do Muslims in London feel? (Jen) Do Muslims change their feelings in a more secular society? How do Christian fundamentalists in the U. S. act? (Tarra)

15. What kind of books are published in Teheran? Are they censored? Who buys books—just the rich? Who reads them? If I bought one who would I be supporting? Is some government encouraging the publication of this book? (Scott)

Period 6

Students read a chapter about family life, religion, and education in the Middle East and answered questions about it for the period. As they worked, I walked around marking the last assignments in the study book and checking the reading and writing assignment they had done the night before. That took about twenty minutes. Then I was free to spend the rest of the class time with one student who couldn't seem to understand the textbook.

Period 7

Another lecture. Students annotated their notes in the right two-inch margin with material from the homework reading for the last two days about religion, family life, arts, and education.

Periods 8 and 9

In their small groups students outlined the best possible group answer to each of the fifteen questions. I was able to spent five to ten minutes with each group each day. Toward the end of Period 9, when the groups were finishing, a representative from each walked down the hall and made copies of the outlines for each member of the group.

Period 10

As students entered the room, a representative from each group drew three tickets from a lottery basket at the front of the room. Each ticket had a number. Then, in order, each group spent two minutes answering questions one through fifteen aloud. After each group answered, the other groups had one minute to add information. All the students filled new information into their personal copies of the outline. These expanded outlines, of course, were taped into the study notebooks.

Period 11

They reported on their interviews; the reports were short summaries and after each a classmate asked one "how did you choose to ask" question. At the end of the period, each group spent ten minutes listing the ten ideas from the interview summaries that were most helpful in answering the original question; they wrote them on an easel sheet and tacked them up on the wall; then the class voted on the ten overall most useful.

It turned out that a lot of students knew someone who had lived or traveled in the Middle East. Their interview questions were about the feelings and values of Muslims. Were they all ready to terrorize people as they walked out of Penguin Bookstores? How would they feel if we bought a book? Of course, they heard many conflicting answers.

For the last couple of minutes, I explained the process for the final demonstrations and told them to outline and practice their answers to the original question.

Periods 12 and 13

As students entered the room, they each drew a colored ticket from the lottery basket, six colors for the six final discussion groups. Then, with a great show of suspense, I picked the order of groups by drawing colored tickets from another basket. The discussions were held in a small conference room near the classroom. The same community member participated both days. At the scheduled time, each group got up and quietly walked to the conference room.

I stayed with the remaining students. Many of them worked quietly at their desks, putting their study notebooks in order to turn in on the last day. They had to make sure all asssigments were included. They filled out a self-rating scale based on the skills, attitudes, and knowledge taught in the unit. They also wrote narrative evaluations to the questions "How were you most successful in preparing this unit?" "How will you work differently next unit?" "What else do you want me to know?" At one time or another, each study group got together and practiced a twenty-minute discussion.

The most time-consuming part of the unit was the final demonstrations. Getting volunteers was easy, as always. I already had a list of possibilities and I have a volunteer training manual (see Appendix). What took the most time were the actual discussions. They were videotaped and I had to watch them at home. My final assessment for this class took about five hours. The students' score was the total of my assessment and the community member's.

However, throughout the unit, I had spent almost no time grading, about three hours total outside of class responding to the study notebooks, and less than eight hours preparing—that's about five hours a week average. I hadn't even spent time with quizzes, since I could always tell who read the assignment well by listening to the small groups.

Period 14

The entire class sat in a circle with their study notebooks on their laps. For the first half of the period, they listed the best and worst aspects of the discussions. Every ten minutes, I stopped and asked students to write down which of the items mentioned applied to them individually. The last half of the class, students wrote self-evaluations. As they left the room, I collected their study notebooks, shook their hands, and congratulated each one enthusiastically.

Where Was Becky?

Becky had been almost invisible throughout the unit. At one point I overheard her expressing surprise that cosmetics were tested on animals: "Do they really put chemicals in their eyes?" Otherwise, she followed instructions and fulfilled assignments, carefully, but not noticeably. When she left the classroom for the final discussion, she was trembling. I was afraid she was going to erupt into tears and refuse to participate. So I was amazed when I saw her videotape.

Becky's first words, as she glanced down at her neck, were, "I wear a cross, but I am a Jew"; she talked about her own struggles with religion and the religious tradition of her family. She put herself in the place of the traditional Muslim and in the place of Rushdie. She used details about the religion, history, and culture of the Arabian Gulf, authoritatively. Finally, she concluded that she would buy the book in New York to assert her belief in free speech and fulfill her responsibilty to seek information and make choices. If she lived in Teheran, though, she wouldn't buy the book because she would be an Arab. Her world view would be different; she would not have the same value for free speech and individual responsiblity; she would have learned to do what her family and social group did. If she were herself in Teheran, not a young Arab woman, she still wouldn't buy the book out of respect for a totally different world view, at least until she had time to understand it firsthand. And she backed up those general statements with facts, examples, and conclusions from the readings, lectures, and group activities.

Becky had learned that school can be safe and active. It's safe to take intellectual and social risks in class, to experiment with adult problems. A class that is organized around actual, adult issues should have all the appeal of a good game, like chess or Monopoly or Dungeons and Dragons. There are rules and limits that keep you safe; but you can experiment with real issues of war, money, or power. School should be better than those games because it lets you practice all of the difficult work of adulthood.

Becky could be a more committed student because she entered a different climate: a serious, busy environment dedicated to excellence. To establish the climate, you really don't have to change much. In fact, you shouldn't change much. We have had fifty years of "major educational change" imposed from the outside by theorists, state education departments, and public pressure; nothing much has changed in the classroom. Teachers are the people who change children. We have always wanted excellence for our students; and most of the elements are already there. All we have to do is restructure slightly toward a more direct goal. My reading assignments are quite traditional; the textbook is a familiar old tome; my lectures are just like many we've all heard before, not particularly original; the information the students acquired, as raw data, was the same old stuff.

What's new is that as soon as you start aiming toward performing adult roles rather than covering material, you have to teach skills and attitudes explicitly. Even the skills are traditional. Mine were lifted straight out of my state syllabus, but they could have come from almost any state: "to perceive and identify the transnational consequences of personal decisions" and "to use speaking skills to persuade." States list attitude objectives too; "intercultural empathy," for example. I was able, though, because of the project approach, to take those skills and attitudes out of the syllabus and put them into the classroom and into Becky.

Becky probably didn't notice; she was too busy answering the questions. What she did notice, though, was the buzzing adolescent energy centered on learning. In a class where the goal is covering the material, students naturally try to meet deadlines and remember the right information. Sameness is prized, not difference; correct is better than interesting; efficiency is more necessary than thoroughness. Minimum competence is accepted. In that system, how could Becky dare to be unique?

In this project, Becky could approach a real problem in her life. Becky's personal question wasn't what I asked; but, since there was no right answer, she could slant her response toward resolving her religious and family conflicts. She didn't answer her own question; but she began to see that she could use history and culture to inform her own life. She also practiced what most effective adults do habitually; they use their own passions and needs to fulfill their responsibilities.

What Becky entered was a learning community, much like the world community we would all like to create: people actively working together to get answers to real questions. The peer pressure was for high achievement; there was no competition because there were no right answers and no "normal curve." Everyone wanted everyone else to succeed just as people on any team want the whole team to win.

It was only December of the ninth grade. Had she entered in May, Becky would have found students working on much more independent questions and projects. There would have been students working at their desks and at computers, before school, after school, and during lunch. Varied projects would have been around the room—maps, charts, outlines, illustrations, and printouts. She would have seen students walking around, complimenting and criticizing. Often, because they take the activities seriously, they are more likely to say, "How did you choose to use that particular chart?" or "I like the way that phrase makes me feel sad" than to throw out a bland "that's good," because they are in the habit of fruitful collaboration.

Actually, Becky didn't see that collaboration in May. By January, she had dropped out of school again. However, she had begun to participate in learning. She was back the following fall. In May of her tenth grade year, she began her unit project, another discussion, with the sentence. "I am a civic humanist; I believe that I should help my community; and I believe that my community is the world."

Chapter Nine

From Here To There
An Alternative School Using Direct Assessment, Epistemic Writing, and Small Groups

When Aaron entered the Academic Community, he got a full guarantee. The community guaranteed that he would achieve high academic standards. All he had to do was participate in its academic life. Aaron didn't know, of course, what this guarantee meant. He didn't understand "participate," nor did he really know what an "academic community" might be. He wouldn't have believed it at first anyway. His earlier experiences in school had taught him a different lesson about what education was, what he was, and what he could be.

The Academic Community for Educational Success is a public alternative program. It helps students develop varied patterns of mind. In the academic courses, naturally, we emphasize academic thinking; there are direct assessments, epistemic writing, and small group activities.

Our "core," the learning that people need for health, welfare, happiness, and citizenship, puts attitudes and skills into students' minds as well as into the syllabus. Conventional schools list goals such as "self-esteem" and "the ability to use analysis and synthesis to understand world affairs"; yet these attitudes and skills are neither taught nor tested there. In most schools, attitudes are primarily part of what Allan Glatthorn (1987) approvingly calls the "soft" curriculum. They are frequently relegated to sports, extracurricular activities, and guidance counseling. Some writing skills are taught explicitly; so are map reading and the scientific method. Most study, communication, and thinking skills, though, are either assumed or ignored. Very few teachers actually teach students to "anticipate" or to "focus"; the major emphasis is on coverage of information. At the Academic Community, skills and attitudes are preeminent, regular, explicit parts of the curriculum.

Most of the "academic" core is organized into intensive "cycles." Some cycles emphasize one discipline; others are transdisciplinary. However, English and communications are involved in all of them. A cycle runs for three consecutive hours a day, Monday through Thursday, for three weeks. If necessary, each cycle can be translated into a conventional "quarter." Biology, for example, is four cycles, global studies, eight. Each three-week cycle receives separate credit.

First, we decide what we want the students to be able to do at the end of each cycle. Then we plan a project that will allow them to demonstrate that they can. Third, we establish standards for the demonstration. Finally, we design learning activities. All learning activities during the three hour time block lead toward this demonstration.

Our cycles emphasize unique achievement through an active, collaborative, academic community. When students work alone, they must be active: if they read, they have to outline, gloss, summarize, question or otherwise demonstrate interaction with their text. When they listen, they take notes. Sometimes they annotate or summarize their notes. Students often work in small groups, developing questions, studying news articles, making lists, formulating documents, outlining procedures, or solving other problems. During breaks or lunch, they practice their speeches and demonstrations on one another. They also use their classmates as audiences for their writing. Everyone's job, students and teachers, is to help each student meet high standards.

During the cycle, students must certainly acquire information, but they can't just memorize. They must connect, reorganize, apply, and evaluate the ideas; so they remember more. They also must learn the attitudes that permit them to study hard and effectively. Finally, in their demonstration, whether it's a speech, a learning log, or a community action, they must demonstrate language, mathematics, communication, and thinking skills as well. The curriculum isn't the least "soft"; it is more, not less, "academic" than most conventional programs because it requires this integration and application of knowledge, attitudes, and skills.

I remember Aaron's first day in our academic community. What I saw was a slender boy with long hair; he seemed quiet and uncertain. Maybe he was hopeful; he was definitely watchful. What he saw (though he didn't recognize it right away) was a new view of school and of himself.

Sometime during his second year Aaron learned that school could be passionate, active, communal, and useful. I first noticed this change in my global studies cycle. I had asked students, "What can you learn about the Soviet Union that will be useful to you in your career or personal life? Pose a question that you want to answer; then prepare a presentation for the school community to share what you have learned about the Soviet Union and about yourself." This time, because the final task was teaching, we looked at examples of excellent teachers. Was the President's State of the Union speech good teaching? How? Martin Luther King's "I had a dream" speech? Bronowski's *Ascent of Man* series?

Students began their study in study teams; they decided what they needed to know about themselves and the Soviet Union. I lectured a couple of times; and they took double-entry notes. They all read about the history and culture of the Soviet Union. A Soviet dissident, now living in our town, told us about leaving the Soviet Union in the sixties. We learned about the role of religion in the Soviet Union by visiting the international headquarters of the Eastern Orthodox Church outside of Russia. We encountered Ukrainian nationalism at a Ukrainian Museum and we ate at a Ukrainian restaurant.

The last week, students regrouped for their presentations. For Aaron, simply acquiring knowledge was easy; if he heard it, he remembered it, at least until the test. However, if remembering data was the point of school, he saw no point in learning. Even as a sixteen year old, Aaron knew that school excellence, judged by percentages right on multiple choice tests, is irrelevant to adult success. Aaron had determined his career goal: to become an antiques dealer. He knew we don't judge antiques dealers by their memories on written tests. Antiques dealers are judged by what they do, what they say, and what they write as well as by what they remember. They are judged by their unique taste and creativity, not by their uniformity. They don't excel because of their broad coverage of information but because of the depth and complexity of their knowledge. Their value is not just in the narrow confines of their one discipline; they are good by the quality of their combined talents: effective salesmanship, superior antiques, attractive display, good advertising, competitive prices, and business management. Until he entered the Academic Community, Aaron's school work was, at best, routine and efficient. He did the minimum so he could pass with a 65 and move on to his "real life."

This assignment allowed him to be passionately involved because he could personalize the topic. He could ask "How has the new Soviet government and economy influenced modern Soviet art?"

Antiques and art are closely connected. Aaron could also be actively responsible for his learning. Together, he and another student went to museums and galleries for slides, read art history and current news, and talked to dealers and curators. They acquired information the way effective adults do, not neatly all in one place from one book and one teacher, but sporadically, by reading, observing, talking, listening, cooperating, questioning, failing, and succeeding. They worked together, also as effective adults do, in a community that valued their particular efforts. Their final performance was not just a test but a personal, passionate, artistic creation.

I don't know exactly when I realized that Aaron had become an active intellectual. Perhaps when he dumped a boxload of art history books onto his desk and asked me to help him and his project partner, Wanda, understand the sophisticated language. Or maybe the day he and Wanda came in and recounted their sad tale of traipsing from museum to museum to see the varied forms of Soviet art. I'm sure I knew as I sat listening to their forty-minute slide show and the subsequent question and answer session. The slender, quiet, watchful boy performed authoritatively and expertly. He went well beyond the coverage and recall required of most high school students. He understood concepts of cubo-futurism and modernism; he was informed about the history and culture of the Soviet Union. He recognized the interdependence of art and culture and talked easily about social realism and *perestroika.* He demonstrated that he could use that information in his everyday life and his future career. Besides, as he showed slides of Kandinsky, Chagall, and Malevich and fluently described their relation to Soviet culture in the twentieth century, his presentation really did approach the expertise of Bronowski.

Aaron also changed his idea of who he was and who he could be through the core courses. Children come to school with a variety of assumptions about the goals of school, the nature of learning, and the characteristics of adulthood. Originally, Aaron felt that there was little relationship between school and his career. He changed that attitude and went on to college. Students also come to school with attitudes toward themselves—high or low self-esteem, helplessness or effectiveness. Aaron felt helpless to change his reading and writing abilities. In conversation after conversation, he explicitly rejected the attitude that people can become more capable through effort. A Book Talk Dinner began to teach him that attitude.

Book Talk Dinners are my favorite literature demonstration projects. One goal of teaching English is to create a community of responders who take personal meaning and pleasure from literature. Literature is a significant ritual for our culture; so another goal is to participate in that ritual. In the United States, we have no common oral tradition or tribal dances. We have no one bard to sing our culture, but we do have many voices to sing our many experiences. We take pleasure in hearing those voices and learning about ourselves in our book talks.

We read novels, short stories, and poetry all year long, of course. Every April, though, for a final demonstration, the students and I choose five somewhat dissimilar books. Maybe one year it will be Jamaica Kincaid's *Annie John*, J. R. Tolkien's *The Hobbit*, John Steinbeck's *The Moon is Down*, Harper Lee's *To Kill a Mockingbird*, and Lore Segal's translation of *The Juniper Tree and Other Tales from Grimm*. About five students choose to read each book. I provide questions; students write long, speculative and reflective essays about their reading. About three weeks later, each book group meets at my home for dinner and conversation with a community member. It's like a literary society or a book club. Our cooking class creates elaborate dinners, matched to the book, Southern chicken and dumplings (with molasses on the side) with *To Kill a Mockingbird* or Caribbean cooking with *Annie John*.

During this activity I can watch students doing the hard work of academic thinking. While they talk, I assess their discussion, holistically, based on educated adults' ways of reading, discussing, and enjoying books. When we discussed *Annie John*, for example, five students met with two community members (a college professor and a high school English teacher, not their own) for three and a half hours. While they ate curried goat and coconut ice, they also rapidly exchanged ideas. They compared different families and cultures, suggested theories of literature, and brought up personal relationships between mothers and daughters. All seven people made choices, questioned themselves and each other, took responsibility for their choices, and subtly altered their ideas. After fourteen years, Book Talks such as *Annie John* have become wonderfully popular. Most students choose to attend more than one Book Talk even though only one is required.

Aaron didn't choose to read more than one book, though; he picked the minimum, probably assuming that he would never read it anyway. One of his first statements when he entered the Academic Community was, "I can't write; I've never been able to write." His immediate response to the Book Talk assignment was "I don't read novels; I've never read an entire novel!" My first response was "What can you do to learn to write?" The second was "What can you do to learn to enjoy novels?" He decided. I started picking him up on the way to school at 6:30 so he could read for an hour and a half before school every morning. Aaron's story is not about magic or miracles. His first Book Talk wasn't excellent. However, between his first Book

Talk, when he didn't quite read the whole book, and his third, two years later, Aaron had many experiences of finding that hard work paid off. His teachers and classmates told him in many ways exactly what skills, attitudes, and habits he needed. His third book talk was superb. In fact, during the third book talk, he sidled up to me and whispered, "He [the community member] didn't even read the whole book; that's insulting to me!" He was genuinely shocked, as I was, that a supposedly responsible person arrived unprepared. Aaron became, through his own efforts and some explicit teaching, a reader and a writer.

Aaron also changed his idea of what he could be. All of his experiences in the cycles obviously contributed to this new perspective. However, it was most apparent through his growing participation in the school government. Sports, counseling, and student government are "curricular" at the Academic Community. These courses are as much a part of the core as social studies, mathematics, science, and English. They are not included in the three week cycles, though. We reserve Fridays for them. We also take many trips for physical education, counseling, and government. These three courses focus on problem solving, decision making, and interpersonal communication. They also emphasize developing positive attitudes and habits toward the community and acquiring personal attitudes of self-esteem and effectiveness.

All students are involved in governing our community. We have a three-part government, with legislative, executive, and judicial branches. There is also a fourth academic branch, similar to the New York State Regents. The students run many aspects of the school. The elected student chief administrator, for example, and his or her cabinet manage attendance and new student admissions as well as school climate, field trips, and a variety of other adminstrative responsibilities. The elected congress makes the rules; the court enforces them. We have to study the U. S. government quite rigorously, of course, to develop our laws and procedures. Students have written and amended a *Constitution* and *Bill of Rights.* Obviously our exemplars are honorable current and historical political leaders. Effective participation is simultaneously a course activity and the final demonstration.

When Aaron entered our school, he had never been involved in school or community activities. He signed our entrance contract which bound him to uphold an honor system and participate fully and responsibly in our community; but his experiences in our community were not immediately idyllic. A new view of your role in the community is as difficult to learn as a new way of being a student.

On one field trip, he violated a major community law. The student court ruled that he had to reconsider and re-sign the contract. It took him several months. As he said, he hadn't really thought about his commitment to the community values the first time he signed. Aaron actually had to confront the values which our country claims, but which many individuals casually violate. Thomas Jefferson, for example, valued the autonomy, dignity, and responsiblity of the individual; but in our country, how many people actually feel personally responsible? He had to weigh the school values against the operating values of his peers. Our honor code stipulates that students won't cheat even on take-home exams and certainly won't steal; it assumes that each individual, like Aaron, would stop or report any incidences of cheating or stealing. Aaron needed an opportunity to analyze, understand, compare, practice, and actively choose his value system. Only through directly and vigilantly confronting such attitudes can we teach them.

By his second year, though, he was appointed to the student court. He learned the attitudes and skills of humane, positive discipline. Through his two-year tenure on that court, he significantly altered the direction of the court and the tone of the school: he developed a control over his own life and influence over the life of his school community. He demonstrated integrity, citizenship, and statesmanship.

At the end of his senior year, as part of the same government course, Aaron ran our scholarhip tag sale, bake sale, and car wash. This project was, of course, a marvelous bridge between his life as student and his future as an antiques dealer. He advertised and collected the merchandise. He also organized twenty-five students to make and distribute signs, work at the sale and car wash, get rid of the debris, clean the building, and resume classes the following Monday without any trace of the tag sale except $1100.

For that same government course, he also demonstrated his ability to contribute personally and constructively to the larger community by spending a weekend working with a youth services organization to feed the homeless in New York City. Aaron had changed his future by changing his idea of what he could be. When the students wrote captions for the yearbook, they put under Aaron's picture, "most likely to be a Yuppie." Aaron laughed because, ironically, it was partly true.

Just a few days ago, Aaron offered to help us with our tag sale. Now he is becomimg an exemplar for our young students. Just before he graduated, Aaron presented our Board of Education with a poetry anthology we had published in English. Aaron wrote the title poem:

Hanging from
The rock
Looking Up at her.

Her hand
Reaching
Clasping mine.

Aaron Liebson

The poem is about risks and resources. It's about falling and rising, needing and getting, loving and accepting love; but for me, it is about Aaron. When he made his presentation, Aaron said "I was diagnosed dysgraphic; but I turned my disability into my ability. I learned to use a few words fully so that each one said a lot."

Aaron learned he could change himself. Through his own effort, he could change his disabilities into his abilities. He learned that the point of school is to give people the power to change. It is the accomplishment that all schools should guarantee.

Chapter Ten

Three Schools
Philosophy for Ordinary People

Three schools—Fayette, Ironton and Lake Osage—all begin with the goal "to teach students to function effectively in a free democratic society." But these three schools are quite different.

Fayette stands on the river bluffs of a midwestern city. Inside, students move quickly through the quiet halls. These students are fully scheduled, five periods a day, with no free time. They only have one elective in their entire four years there. Otherwise, all students take the same required courses, grades nine through twelve, and the same final examinations.

Fayette is proud of its faculty. Many of them got their undergraduate degrees from the university known locally as "the Harvard of the Midwest." By and large, they now have Ph.D.s and impressive lists of publications. These teachers primarily teach. They certainly don't do hall duty or supervise extracurricular activities. No one does. The principal's main role is curriculum leader. Classwork is much more important than discipline, attendance, counseling or after school activities. Fayette is known for the number of merit scholars it produces every year.

Ironton is seven miles away in a glass and steel building, designed by a well-known "school" architect. It's much larger than Fayette, 1700 students instead of 300. Classes are larger. The ratio of adults to students is much lower. As you peek through the Plexiglas classroom doors, you notice that some of the teaching methods are similar to Fayette's: lectures and notes, worksheets and tests. The tone is different though. Teachers are trained in classroom management; they criticize and praise a great deal. The union and the district sponsor workshops in research-based classroom techniques. Also, students are broken into three "homogeneous" levels: general, college-prep, and honors.

Students can choose from many electives, like "popular literature," and "Chinese cooking." Ironton's extracurricular activities are known statewide, particularly drama and music. The Pupil Personnel Services Department has developed extensive drug and suicide prevention programs. Last year, at the awards assembly, the Assistant Principal for Student Affairs gave over four hundred awards varying from "Future Business Leader" to "Outstanding Musician of the Year."

Lake Osage is slightly smaller than Fayette, about 250 students. Unlike both Fayette and Ironton, however, there are no separate departments. Most teachers teach several subjects. Courses are often interdisciplinary. The head teacher coordinates much of the administration, although the thirty or so staff members usually make important administrative decisions together. Students are often involved in those decisions through all-community meetings. Last spring, the head teacher turned down a national award because at Lake Osage, students and staff feel that they all participate in any one person's success and no one member of the community should receive the honors.

You are likely to see small groups of students working on projects together on the front steps or in the large open areas inside. Lake Osage is known for its community apprenticeship program. State requirements are met by individual contracts. There are also no organized drug prevention programs or extracurricular activities. Teachers and students discuss drug and family problems as friends. On many Friday afternoons, students, teachers, and even parents get together for soccer games and picnics on the long back lawn overlooking the lake.

How can Fayette, Ironton, and Lake Osage have the same goal and be so unlike? In fact, their goals are *not* the same. The words "student," "teach," "free," and "function effectively" do not mean the same to these three schools. Their assumptions about human nature, knowledge, and learning are quite different. In other words, their philosophies are different. If the schools are coherent, we should be able to infer these philosophies from their organization, curriculum, and methods. See if you can match each school with an elaborated goal statement:

1. ———'s goal is to teach our students to function effectively in a free democratic society. Each student must be able to fulfill his

intellectual, social, and personal potential. Methods, content, and evaluation must be individualized so that each student may discover his or her own identity and goals. Since each student has an equal right to an education, each student has a right to learn what is best for him or her. The best preparation for adult life is a chance to find personal autonomy and integrity so that citizens may function freely in a pluralistic society.

2. ———'s goal is to teach our students to function effectively in a free democratic society: to be able to make rational decisions at the voting booth, in personal relationships, and in professional activities. Our first priority is to teach them to acquire information about the world, analyze and synthesize this information, and act on their logical conclusions. To this end, we focus on a core of essential information, on the patterns of inquiry characteristic of each discipline, and on the thought processes common to all thinking and learning. Since all students have an equal right to education, they all must master the same information and the same skills. The best preparation for adult life is to learn to think independently and to understand the accumulated wisdom of our culture.

3. ———'s goal is to teach our students to function effectively in a free democratic society. They must learn the values and traditions of that society; they must learn to cooperate and compromise in order to work together. Because our society comprises many subcultures and disparate values, we must not only teach them shared values and appropriate social behavior, but also provide them many options for learning different subjects. Since all students have an equal right to an education, the high school will provide many methods and levels, as well as specific electives, appropriate to different students' needs. The best preparation for adult life is for students to master the courses appropriate to their future adult studies or careers.

Goal number 1 is Lake Osage's. Its policies are based on the romanticism of Jean Jacques Rousseau and Bronson Alcott and the individualism of Ralph Waldo Emerson. Reality is in the mind. People are creatures of sentiment rather than reason; intuition and imagination rather than logic; will rather than intellect. Development means the natural flowering of personality. Knowledge is growing self-image, self-discovery, and self-determination. The metaphor is biological. Children develop through natural stages like plants. Lake Osage's primary goal, then, is to encourage individuals to fulfill their potential. The teacher's role is to cultivate the students' natural creativity, intuition, and expressiveness without interfering with their personal liberty. A good school is one in which children are happy, healthy, creative, and confident. "Effective citizens" are the ones who can fulfill their personal destinies.

Fayette holds goal number 2. It's the little citadel of John Locke and René Descartes. It's based on the philosophy of the Enlightenment. Just as there was a physical order in Newton's world, there was a social order in Locke's. Reality exists outside the human mind; some order is out there *á priori*. People are basically rational. By careful observation and mathematical reasoning, they can discover that order. Initially, the mind is a blank tablet that receives sensory impressions and experiential data. Gaining knowledge is gathering this data and sorting information into logical structures. The main goal is to teach children to make rational judgments. The method is to provide information and practice. Since learning is essentially reactive rather than formative, students are passive listeners, observers, and memorizers. Teachers "contain" information. They lecture, they assign reading, and they test acquisition of knowledge. Disciplines are "content areas"; physics, history, and literature each have basic truths that teachers pass on to students. Students memorize dates in United States history and learn the meaning of communism. "Objective" evaluation methods measure the students' accomplishments. A "good school" is one with high S.A.T.s, a lot of merit scholars, high college placements, and teachers with advanced degrees. An effective citizen has sufficient data and can reason scientifically.

Goal 3 is Ironton's. Its philosophical base is a behaviorist or utilitarian model like Bentham's Panopticon. The utilitarians did not believe in eternal truths. People are motivated by feelings. Their reasoning is based on seeking pleasure and avoiding pain. Ordinary people do *not* usually make reasoned decisions based on data and long-term goals. Instead, an enlightened administrator has to govern them, particularly children and other dependents, to prevent them from hurting one another. So the school has a high proportion of administrators to supervise, evaluate, and reward teachers. Similarly, the enlightened teacher's role is to control and train the students. Therefore, there's an emphasis on classroom management techniques. For students, development means becoming more socialized.

One of Ironton's primary roles is to teach shared values and social responsiblity. Ironton emphasizes uniformity and discourages divergent thought. Ironton's primary method, because people are motivated by pleasure and pain, is external rewards—grades and honors. Students are tracked into low-level, job-oriented, hands-on courses or into professional sequences according to the role most appropriate to them. In this industrial model, a good school is an efficient, clean, orderly, and quiet place. "Effective citizens" are those who recognize and fulfill their roles.

Fayette, Ironton, and Lake Osage differ in organization, curriculum, and methods because they differ in metaphysics, ethics, and epistemology. Philosophy is our basic thoughts about life rather than our particular thoughts about the parts of life. Disciplines like science and history are structured thoughts about the parts of life. Science formulates hypotheses and conclusions about the physical parts. A historian investigates relationships of people, events, and institutions through time and forms conclusions about connections. A philosopher asks more ultimate questions: "What is human nature?" "What are knowledge and learning?" Both science and history, though, depend on our answers to these more fundamental, philosophical questions.

So do all of our educational decisions. The basis of education is our definition of what adults in the United States *should be* and *can be;* that is, our philosophy. Often we forget that our educational system does not stand separate from our beliefs. It grows from them.

Fayette, Ironton, and Lake Osage primarily exist in our minds, of course. Occasionally small alternative schools and small private schools do have such consistent philosophies. Currently, Lake Osage has some real counterparts in a few public alternative schools across the country and, historically, in the "free schools" or "open schools" of the sixties. Similarly, Fayette has some analogues among private prep schools. In general, Ironton, however, represents the dominant philosophy of the familiar comprehensive high school, the one we've all known since James Conant's *The American High School Today* (1959). Real comprehensive public schools, however, never have so consistent a philosophy as Ironton. More often these "shopping mall high schools" (Powell 1985) represent the many beliefs of their communities. Basically, they are set up on an empirical and rational model; they combine Ironton and Fayette. There is also a sprinkling of Lake Osage, though. We like to think, for example, that we educate "the whole child." We employ "the process approach" to writing and encourage "the divine fire" in art and poetry.

In addition to the hodgepodge of these three philosophies, a variety of other philosophies exist in our comprehensive high schools. Although many Americans believe we know the world primarily through our minds, others believe that truth comes from prayer and sacred books and that divine truth supersedes empirical truth. While our teaching methods in public schools don't depend on divine revelation, there is real conflict over the "truths" we teach: What theories of creation should be presented? What is the place of prayer in schools? In fact, many colonial schools were religious institutions. The "Little Jug" School House, a one room school dating from 1829, still stands in my hometown. Students learned to read there by reading the *Bible.* Across this country, many people still keep the Little Jug or even more specifically religious schools in their minds as educational models.

None of these four types of school represents John Dewey either. Yet Dewey's pragmatism has provided some of the most influential school models of any philosophy. For Dewey, there is no goal in society; there are no absolutes. What we aim for is simply continued development. Freedom and our other national values are only the best means to a good life in this world. There is no eternal truth—not in science, not in philosophy, not in day-to-day living—only more effective ways of dealing with problems. All knowledge is relative and historic. For Dewey, the process is important, not the goal. For him, traditional philosophy provides fake solutions. Instead, we should aspire to control the phenomenal world through science. The learner is neither a blank tablet nor a developing plant; knowledge is neither totally outside the learner nor is it totally determined by the natural stages of growth within the child. It develops from the inter- action of a child's mind and the world's events. Learning is dialecti- cal changes in the patterns of mind through experience. Students are more like athletes toning their intellectual muscles and acquiring knowledge necessary to their sports. They are active and involved in their learning. As they acquire information and skills, their knowl- edge changes their perception of the world, and their experience changes their intellectual patterns.

Teachers are more coaches than farmers, lecturers, or managers. They create environments for students to use information, practice skills, overcome obstacles, and solve problems. Although teachers may help select some essential information, they don't completely organize it for their students. Instead, they encourage students to interact with information directly. Dewey's pragmatism exists in classes that focus on experiential learning; students do problem-solv- ing activities, study original documents, and get information through interviews. The Bank Street School for Children in New York City (Mitchell 1950) was founded on the philosophy of John Dewey.

The difficulty is that we accept the truth of all these beliefs— Rousseau, Locke, Bentham, the *Bible,* and Dewey—unconsciously; these "truths" often seem mutually incompatible. Christopher Lasch feels that the aims of mass education which result from Locke's and Bentham's philosphies—informed and conforming citizens—

undermine one another. Thus, Fayette and Ironton are philosophical opposites. For A. S. Neill (1960), individual liberty cannot coexist with enforced intellectual discipline *or* intentional enculturation. That is, Lake Osage is antithetical to both Ironton and Fayette. And, although they are incompatible, Lake Osage, Fayette, and Ironton exist jumbled together with the Little Jug and Bank Street School in our comprehensive high schools. Is analytic reasoning more important than enculturation or self-actualization? Our culture has never decided. Sometimes we have held one view of development, sometimes another. Often some social need seems to determine which philosophy is dominant. The "immigrants" for whom Calvin Woodward created "life adjustment" education were quite different from the ones that Thomas Jefferson dealt with a hundred years earlier. Thomas Jefferson was writing about immigrants who shared with him the English cultural, legal, and political traditions. By 1850, Americans felt that the immigrants had to be "Americanized." Educators had to teach them not only civic values and obligations, but also obedience, politeness, and cleanliness. Schools like Ironton began to develop then. In the 1960s, the time of Sputnik, the tension was once again between the two educational poles of *Hard Times* in the 1850s—rigid academics or "free schools." Empirical rationalism, utilitarianism, romanticism, theism, and pragmatism, these five philosophies always lie below the surface of our educational policies to reemerge in response to some current social need.

We come to our classes with unconscious preconceptions about learning, knowledge, and human nature. Our cultural heritage and our personal educational experiences built Fayette, Ironton, Lake Osage, the Little Jug, and Bank Street in our collective national mind. These hidden assumptions work against one another in our districts and our classrooms. Most of the time, we don't even consider that they might conflict.

Districts, schools, departments, and committees apparently make choices on a short-term perception of "what works" without explicitly articulating "works to do what?" Our Curriculum Council chooses a computerized attendance system because another district has used it with "success." What kind of person does a computerized attendance system help to develop? Or maybe we choose what we need to solve an immediate political problem. The Board of Education, for example, offers driver's education so that vocal parents can get lower insurance rates. Maybe we require more social studies so a popular young social studies teacher won't lose her job or develop a writing program because the papers are crying about the lowered writing ability of graduates. What could we have had instead of drivers ed, more social studies, and a writing program? What impact might a different choice have had on what our students could do after they graduate? All of the members of the Curriculum Council, the Board of Education, the social studies department and the English department are unconsciously operating from assumptions about what students should and can be and do. Those fundamental assumptions, however, are never part of our debates.

Suppose you're on the Board of Education in your district. Which program do you choose to spend eighty thousand dollars on?

	Plan 1	Plan 2	Plan 3
$30,000	a social worker to develop and implement a suicide prevention program	a resident poet and a resident filmmaker to work with interested students on their self-expression in poetry and film	a study-lab teacher to help students who have difficulty with physics
$50,000	An assistant principal to follow up on attendance problems	$1^{1}/_{2}$ teachers to facilitate the development of individual projects for students	a pre-K program for children who need extra preparation for school

If you picked Plan 1, Ironton's glass and steel structure probably stands strongest in your mind. Plan 2 is consistent with Lake Osage and Plan 3 with Fayette. Most of us would have chosen without considering what model dominated our thinking. Ultimately, every choice is philosophical. All the piecemeal choices taken together, though, constitute the school philosophy—stated or unstated, coherent or incoherent. Most of our group choices are incoherent and even conflicting.

Similarly, all our classroom decisions coalesce into our effective classroom philosophy. The goal of education, after all, is to change people whether "change" means "develop innate abilities," "socialize," or even "extirpate evil." Our philosophy is simply a clear definition of what we want students to be. When we choose a book or an activity, we choose, in part, our students' futures.

Teachers often arrange students at separate desks or carrels to work "at their own pace." What future are we choosing? Is the teacher choosing a management technique to maintain order and get the most "time on task" out of the "allocated time" as he would at Ironton? Does he have an idea of letting the individual develop his personal creative genius as he might at Lake Osage? Is the effect to teach children to be "individualistic" or alone? Will they become independent problem-solvers or passive, dependent followers? Similarly, the way teachers present the United States government could either transfer their definitions of "checks and balances" into passive learners or it could model critical thinking. Do your teaching strategies work against one another?

If we unconsciously think we're teaching empty vessels, we may produce dependent and passive, if knowledgeable, citizens. If we treat students as if we can only cultivate the soil they grow in, we may sow ignorance. If we teach them that the world is purely a problem to be solved, they will not necessarily value their cultural heritage. Yet often we don't even consider whether we're trying to fill empty vessels, let the little buds blossom or coach mental gymnasts. We choose our curriculum and organization without considering our ethics and metaphysics and our methods without acknowledging our epistemology.

If our educational leaders have not chosen a philosophy in two hundred years, they probably won't do so in our lifetimes. Meanwhile we're in an untenable position. If we have the hubris to claim to alter children's minds, to influence their specific attitudes, knowledge, and skills, we have the ethical responsibility to know exactly what we want them to become. As individuals, at least, we must begin by considering our goals carefully. Our responses to state-mandated curricula, to popular educational movements, or to individual students' problems cannot be idiosyncratic, fragmented, or counterproductive.

It's hard to formulate a classroom philosophy. I can easily construct an educational philosophy for a small school in an isolated community—a commune, for example, like Koinonia partners in Americas, Georgia. At least Koinonia's community purpose seems clear: to establish "a partnership with God and people everywhere." In Koinonia there is a shared philosophy.

But my public school classroom represents the United States; and the United States of America is not Americas, Georgia. Our national koinonia includes Bedford, New York, a metropolitan suburb, and Berne, Indiana, a farming community with Swiss Mennonite roots, as well as Americas, Georgia, itself. In our national educational heritage stand Ironton, Fayette, Lake Osage, the Little Jug, the Bank Street School, and many others.

All of us, in order to develop a coherent classroom, must identify which of these mental schools we want our classroom in. The way to find that philosophy is to paint one more picture. We need to envision what we want our students to be capable of being and doing when they finish our classes. Over the last few years, I have been painting these portraits. They hang invisible on my classroom wall and I score my classroom activities against them just as I score students holistically against exemplars. They're successful students I've taught. As I run into former students, I occasionally add a portrait. I hung a new one just a few weeks ago.

I had to have a plaque engraved this year. It was to commemorate the twenty students who'd won a Citizenship Essay Contest in the last twenty years. The district had no record of the award for one year. I started calling around. Several people thought it might have been Kimmie, the student who described the Kikuyus as "noisy, disgusting little varmints." When I reached Kim, she assured me she had got it, "The certificate is right in my room," she said. She also said, "I never thought I'd see my name on a plaque."

When Kim was in my tenth grade social studies class, she was already abusing drugs. She did go to college, but didn't finish. Sometime during her sophomore year, she woke up one Saturday in a rat-infested apartment in New York City, surrounded by people she'd never seen before. Right after that, she went to a drug rehabilitation center for several months. After she was released, she continued with outpatient drug counseling, started a small catering business with one of her mom's friends, and went to school part time. That was the last I heard of her until my phone conversation. Kim's most exciting news was that she'd finished her degree and was working at Greens' Farms, the same drug rehab she'd been too. She was a psychologist and drug counselor.

What matters isn't just what students are in school but where they will be when they're thirty-five. Graduation is too soon. All we can expect at graduation is demonstrated potential. Kim came to kindergarten with personal and cultural disadvantages, from a home rather like Laura's. She was an erratic student in high school. In fact, she was still uncertain and unhappy when she graduated, the same year she won that certificate.

Now she has the adult qualities I want to build toward in my classes. Kim is empathetic with other people and aware of their feelings toward her. The little girl who thought unfamiliar customs were barbaric has now learned to put herself in others' places. You can tell by the way she talks about her family, clients, and colleagues. Andy, even though he cared about me and others, never did understand my feelings about that Christmas tree. Kim, though, talks articulately about her unsuccessful marriage and her ex-husband's misperception of what she was. She still seems to have an amicable, cooperative relationship with him, though. She is confident that she is admired by her colleagues at Greens' Farms, and she feels valued in her neighborhood as well. She belongs. She is secure, even in the context of all the difficulties she's had.

Most important to me, she is powerful. She knows how to use information and skills to make choices and take actions. She's a lifelong student. When I talked to her, she wanted to know about her old classmates, of course. But she also wanted to know about my work. What books did I read? What psychologists did I like? She asked to read this book. Back in tenth grade, I helped her become a historian and a sociologist in the way that academicwise people can be. She now observes her seven-year-old son's interactions with her family and his peers, she studies about children and parenting, and she has investigated her family history to calculate the likelihood that her boy also will be drug prone. She analyzes, connects, and synthesizes. She's excited when she's created a new idea and is often driven to take action. She's passionate. She volunteered on the phone to come back to our district to do drug counseling.

Kimmie doesn't let the world just happen to her. She doesn't just sit in front of the television or behind a book and let the experience pass through her. She uses information to keep growing. She doesn't let addiction, divorce, and poverty destroy her. She seeks experiences and those experiences change her. She's skilled, knowledgeable, committed, and active.

When I'm teaching, I can look up at that imaginary portrait and measure my current decisions against it. What did I do with Kimmie? How would I describe the philosophical and methodological classroom environment that helped nurture these qualities in Kim?

If I had to sketch the imaginary building that my classroom would be in, I suppose it would be primarily a John Dewey school, with a touch of Fayette. I think I believe in absolutes; at least I passionately want freedom, equality, justice, and happiness to exist for my students. I believe that one way to acquire those ideals is through our cultural heritage. Our culture has provided us with powerful patterns of mind: symbolic thought, artistic thought, musical thought, spatial thought, and academic thought. Our students should learn those patterns in school to augment their opportunities for freedom, equality, justice, and happiness. To that extent, parts of my classroom come from Fayette.

My methods, though, sit solidly in a Dewey school. Certainly, our students must acquire attitudes, information, and skills. They learn them, however, by interacting with the world, by focusing on what they want to do and learning to do it through practice. Direct assessments, epistemic writing, small groups, and students' projects all contribute to that interaction. Freedom, to me, means the power of choice. An effective citizen is one who can choose.

When Andy, Dave, Don, and Laura leave high school, each, like Kimmie, Jennifer, and Aaron, should have this power: to consider, judge, and choose a way of life. All six should be more free from the limits of their own backgrounds—personal, social, and intellectual. They should be capable of meeting the challenges of work or college because they have self-esteem, confidence, and persistence. They should be able to deal with the physical world because they know science, mathematics, and language. They should be able to meet their obligations to themselves, their families, and their world because they have a historical and cross-cultural understanding of individuals, systems, and world views. They should be able to perpetuate their culture because they understand and value it. They should also be able to take lifelong pleasure, pride, and learning from their global heritage: from Plato and Thomas Aquinas, from Galileo and Lao-Tse, from Sojourner Truth, Maimonides, and Confucius.

That goal must be acomplished by all of us working together. My share occurs in English and history courses in a small Northeastern town. My colleagues do their share all over the United States. Together, we have a profound responsiblity. In 1900 fewer than seven percent of seventeen year olds graduated from high school; elementary school was preparation for adulthood. In another hundred years, maybe college will be. Right now, however, near the year 2000, we are the ones who educate people for adulthood.

Thomas Jefferson described effective citizens as people who can't be fooled by oratory or bullied by authority because of their dignity and rationality. We owe all our students that dignity and rationality.

Chapter Eleven

Where the Mind is Without Fear

A Sacred Trust

Where the mind is without fear and the head is
  held high
Where knowledge is free . . .
Where tireless striving stretches the arms toward
  perfection;
Where the clear stream of reason has not lost its
  way into the dreary desert sand of dead
  habits
My father

  let my country awake

Rabindranath Tagore, 1913

Common sense is the way we usually think. When we arrange the dishes in the kitchen cabinet, plan Saturday nights, or choose a book to read, we ordinarily accept the traditions and habits of our community. Essentially, we deal daily with the physical and social world without much reflection or additional information. Most of us even go a bit out of our way to avoid questioning our assumptions. But then something happens. We read an article in the paper about people eating dogs or we are suddenly afraid we will die in a nuclear disaster or someone directs sexist or racist language toward us. What do we do?

Laura retreats into a loud reaffirmation of commonsense attitudes. She really has no other choice because she does not know there are other ways to think. Kimmie has other resources. Unlike Laura, Kimmie has had three years of classes that emphasized practice in academic thinking.

In her junior and senior years, I had many chances to observe Kimmie's growth. I heard about one of these demonstrations of academic thinking while she was in eleventh grade. Both Kimmie and Laura grew up near an area increasingly populated by immigrants from Central America. In that neighborhood there were major economic and housing problems. The Latino immigrants often lived in crowded, unsanitary apartments. When Kim walked to the bus in the morning, she was frightened by the agricultural workers who stood near her corner waiting for a ride to the farms and orchards upstate. Sometimes they called out to her. The common belief in her neighborhood was that they should be shipped back where they came from.

In her U. S. history class, she heard two presentations; the first was given by people involved in the sanctuary movement and the second by a representative of the U. S. Immigration and Naturalization Service. In the first, a young illegal alien told horror stories about the persecution of his brothers in El Salvador; he said that the U. S. government suppressed information about El Salvador and refused to give his people political asylum because the U. S. government would look bad if they acknowledged that a government they supported persecuted its citizens. He also described his personal misery and degradation at living in the United States illegally. He couldn't get a job; he had to sleep in a filthy room with three other men; and he had to suffer the contempt and hatred of many Americans who didn't want him on their streets. Although they weren't assigned, Kim took home his materials and read them assiduously. The next week the immigration official presented a forceful, and antithetical, argument. Kimmie went to her teacher with distress puffing up her face. "He lied to me," she said, meaning the Salvadorean she'd found so convincing; and her teacher said, "How do you know?" For several months, she occasionally asked the teacher questions about El Salvador, immigration laws, and the Sanctuary movement. The last quarter of her senior year, Kim had to develop a social action project for her government course. She designed and implemented a tutorial and support program for schoolchildren who didn't speak English. She and three of her classmates worked in a nearby elementary school, primarily with Latino children.

I don't know what conclusion Kimmie finally drew about how to deal with the Latino people she encountered. I know that when she came to a question that common sense didn't address, she was able to use academic thinking to approach the issue. In her academic classes, she was able to develop three attitudes that allowed her to behave differently from Laura. First, she could pull back and question her own traditions and habits: "What's really happening here? Where did my ideas come from? What's really right?" She could detach herself enough from her preconceptions to review and possibly change them. Second, she could believe that more information and skills were valuable. She believed that there were ideas, feelings, and events that she had never known. She could imagine the Latino people's and the immigration officer's thoughts even though she had little experience with either. Finally, she was justifiably confident that she had the academic skills to find, sort, organize, appraise, and above all, use that information.

By observing Kimmie and Laura and hundreds of other students in English, science, and social studies classes, I have come to realize that the original metaphor in *Schoolwise* was misleading, both to my readers and me. Teaching is not at all like driving a car. Minds are not like engines; they cannot be divided into mechanical parts and understood; they do not operate by inviolable laws. We certainly can't fill them up with history, physics, literature, and mathematics, and know that it will give them power to get to the end of the trip. That metaphor was chosen from a "cultural transmission" model. I wrote the first draft of Chapter 1 many years ago, before I started my research. *Schoolwise* began with a genuine question to discuss with my colleagues and to investigate in my classes. I kept the original metaphor as evidence of the way I have changed.

In the many years since that first sentence, I've learned that while teaching may stall, children's minds do not, in fact, break down. There was nothing wrong with Laura's mind. She simply never acquired a useful way of understanding. Laura never learned that central lesson, that there was a way of thinking that could answer important questions and solve pressing problems. Laura was left resentful and angry at people she didn't know and couldn't understand. Kimmie became substantially different by acquiring a new pattern of mind.

Our students can be tyrannized, or liberated, by the way they think. Their eyes, ears, and hands can only see, hear, and feel by inference. Dignity, equality, power, health, and happiness depend on choices they can imagine and actions they can take. When we teach academic thinking, we give children choices: power to resist oppression; tools to improve their health and comfort; and relative (though never total) freedom from the limitations of their birth. Through academic thinking, they can see and make a different world; they can create their roles in society rather than lose their way in the "dreary desert sand of dead habits."

If we don't teach academic thinking or if we teach *only* academic thinking, we limit those choices. In our Western culture there are other equally important patterns of mind. And, as Fritjof Capra reminds us, there are also patterns of mind beyond our Western heritage (1982). Yet intellectual freedom through academic thinking preserves all other pathways to wisdom. It allows us to step out of our preconceptions and to recognize other patterns of mind. It is our sacred trust, then, to teach academic thinking and to take young people "Where the mind is without fear and the head is held high/ Where knowledge is free . . ./ Where tireless striving stretches the arms toward perfection."

Appendix: Direct Assessments

Scoring Instructions and Rating Scale

Each assessment is holistic. The tasks are complex intellectual challenges. They involve control over the specific "know-how" and "know-what" of global studies and U. S. history and government; they also depend on general thinking skills such as reading, writing, speaking, listening, analyzing, synthesizing, patterning, predicting, and judging.

The purpose of assessment is to show you and the students what they can do. It's not to show you what they don't know. Therefore, there's no one right answer; there are many possible good solutions.

You should read the course goals and key concept sheet carefully. They give an overview of what the students have been studying; the students must use some of the specific information implied by these concept sheets, but no one could use it all.

Under no circumstances, however, should students simply repeat undigested facts or definitions; they should have integrated the information into a coherent, useful pattern. Ask open-ended question, not simply recall questions, in order to let the students show you that they can pattern the information and put it to use.

Please evaluate each student individually. Achievement on these tasks is not competitive and should not be scored on a curve.

You should observe, read, or hear the students' demonstrations and give a quick holistic response based on the following categories:

EXCELLENT = 6 points: The student's response is complete, clear, coherent, and accurate. She has understood and organized the task well. She actively uses many of the key concepts and specifies people, places, times, events, and ideas. She uses both broad concepts and particular data well to defend an opinion, solve a problem, or complete a task. This response has many of the characteristics of the response you would expect from an expert in the field; it shows mastery of the discipline's vocabulary and methods of inquiry. The student demonstrates excellence in communication and in reasoning. The student quite possibly uses visual aids, dramatic methods, and appropriate tools. In other words, this response is distinguished by particular expertise, uniqueness, or creativity.

GOOD = 5 points: The student gives a fairly complete and accurate response. He has understood and defined the task. He uses some of the key concepts and specifies them. However, he does not use so many effectively. He uses them appropriately, though, to defend an opinion, solve a problem, or complete a task. This response shows familiarity with the vocabulary and methods of inquiry of the field, if not mastery. The student also reads or writes clearly and reasons effectively. The presentation is well-organized.

SATISFACTORY = 4 points: The student defends the opinion, solves the problem, or completes the task. However, she uses isolated specifics without understanding the overall pattern or she discusses the concepts without grounding them in specifics. Her familiarity with the vocabulary and inquiry methods of the discipline are limited; her communication skills or reasoning patterns may be flawed.

INSUFFICIENT = 3 points: The student just barely fails to defend the opinion, solve the problem, or complete the task. He mentions a few of the concepts and a few specific facts, but clearly is not in command enough of either to be effective. He shows awareness of the vocabulary and inquiry methods of the discipline, but cannot use them well; his communication skills may be limited or reasoning patterns muddled.

UNSATISFACTORY = 2 points: The student may understand the problem. She tries to address the issues, but still does not defend the opinion, solve the problem, or complete the task.

UNACCEPTABLE = 1 point: The student misunderstands the problem; he does not address the issues. He does not understand the goal of his response nor is he able to really begin.

NO RESPONSE = 0 points: The student makes no attempt at all. She is absent, silent, or submits blank paper.

For each assessment, there will be at least two scorers, the teacher and a qualified outside evaluator. The student's combined score will indicate the final grade.

Excellent = 10–12

Satisfactory = 7–9

Unsatisfactory = 0–6

In the case of a difference between the two scores of greater than three points, the assessment should be repeated or reviewed by a second outside evaluator.

Works Cited

Allen, Woody. 1975. *Without Feathers.* New York: Ballantine Books.

Bateson, Gregory. 1979. *Mind and Nature: A Necessary Unity.* New York: E. P. Dutton.

Bernstein, Basil. 1979. "Social Class, Language and Socialization." In Lee, Victor (ed)., *Language Development.* New York: John Wiley & Sons.

Berry, Mary F., and John W. Blassingame. 1982. *Long Memory: The Black Experience in America.* New York: Oxford University Press.

Bloom, Benjamin S. (ed). 1956. *Taxonomy of Educational Objectives: The Classification of Educational Goals. Handbook I: Cognitive Domain.* New York: David McKay Company.

Bruner, Jerome. 1960. *The Process of Education.* New York: Vintage Books.

Bruner, Jerome. 1986. *Actual Minds, Possible Worlds.* Cambridge, MA: Harvard University Press.

Capra, Fritjof. 1982. *The Turning Point: Science, Society, and the Rising Culture.* New York: Bantam Books.

Cole, Michael, and Barbara Means. 1981. *Comparative Studies of How People Think.* Cambridge, MA: Harvard University Press.

Coles, Robert. 1990. "The Moral Life of America's Schoolchildren." *Teacher Magazine* (March): 42–49.

Costa, Arthur. 1985. *Developing Minds: A Resource Book for Teaching Thinking.* Alexandria, VA: Association for Supervision and Curriculum Development.

Dansereau, D.F., and K.W. Collins; B.A. McDonald; C.D. Holley; J. Garland; G. Diekoff; S.H. Evans. 1979. "Development and Evaluation of a Learning Strategy Training Program." *Journal of Educational Psychology* 71:64–73.

de Bono, Edward. [1971] 1985. *Practical Thinking.* New York: Viking Penguin Inc.

de Bono, Edward. 1982. *DeBono's Thinking Course.* New York: Facts on File Publications.

Dewey, John. [1916] 1966. *Democracy and Education: An Introduction to the Philosophy of Education.* New York: Free Press.

Dewey, John. [1938] 1963. *Experience and Education.* New York: The Macmillan Company.

diSessa, Andrea A. 1981. *Phenomenology and the Evolution of Intuition.* The Division for Study and Research in Education Working Papers. Cambridge, MA: Massachusetts Institute of Technology.

Ennis, R.H. 1975. "An Alternative to Piaget's Conceptualization of Logical Competence." *Child Development* 47:903–919.

Erikson, Erik H. 1964. *Childhood and Society.* New York: W. W. Norton, Inc.

Feuerstein, Reuven. 1980. *Instrumental Enrichment: An Intervention Program for Cognitive Modifiability.* Baltimore: University Park Press.

Flower, Linda. 1979. "Writer-Based Prose: A Cognitive Basis for Problems in Writing." *College English* 41:19–37.

Freud, Sigmund. 1989. *General Selection from the Works of Sigmund Freud.* New York: Doubleday & Co., Inc.

Gardner, Howard. 1983. *Frames of Mind: The Theory of Multiple Intelligences.* New York. Basic Books, Inc.

Glatthorn, Allan A. 1987. *Curriculum Leadership.* Alexandria, VA: Association for Supervision and Curriculum Development.

Gombrich, E.H. 1965. "Artistic Representation." in Jerome Stolnitz. *Aesthetics.* New York: The MacMillan Company.

Goodlad, John I. 1984. *A Place Called School: Prospects for the Future.* New York: McGraw-Hill Book Company.

Gregorc, Anthony F. 1979. "Learning Styles: Differences Which the Profession Must Address." in R. Vacca and J. Meagher (eds). Storrs, Ct.: The University of Connecticut.

Guilford, J. P. 1967. *The Nature of Human Intelligence.* New York: McGraw-Hill.

Guilford, J. P., and R. Hoeptner. 1971. *The Analysis of Intelligence.* New York: McGraw-Hill.

Hallam, Roy N. 1970. "Logical Thinking in History." In Martia Ballard (ed.) *New Movements in the Study and Teaching of History.* Bloomington: Indiana University Press.

Hirsch, E. D., Jr. et al. 1988. *The Dictionary of Cultural Literacy: What Every American Needs to Know.*, Boston: Houghton Mifflin.

Hofstader, Douglas. 1979. *Goedel, Escher, and Bach.* New York: Basic Books.

Kohlberg, Lawrence. 1972 "Development as the Aim of Education." *Harvard Education Review* 42:449–496.

———. 1981. *Moral States and the Idea of Justice. Volume One: Essays on Moral Development.* New York: Harper & Row.

Kuhn, T. S. 1962. *The Structure of Scientific Revolutions.* Chicago: University of Chicago Press.

Labov, William. 1979. "The Logic of Nonstandard English." In Lee, Victor (ed). *Language Development.* New York: John Wiley & Sons.

Lipman, M., and A. Sharp; F Oscanyan. 1980. *Philosophy in the Classroom.* 2nd ed. Philadelphia: Temple University Press.

Lochhead, J., and Clement. J. (Eds.). 1979. *Cognitive Process Instruction: Research on Teaching Thinking Skills.* Philadelphia, PA: Franklin Institute Press.

Lockwood, Alan L., and David E. Harris. 1985. *Reasoning with Democratic Values: Ethical Problems in United States History.* Vols. I & II. New York: Teachers College Press.

Mitchell, Lucy Sprague. 1950. *Our Children and Our Schools: A Picture and Analysis of How Today's Public Schools' Teachers Are Meeting the Challenge of New Knowledge and New Cultural Needs.* New York: Simon and Schuster.

———. 1971. *Young Geographers.* New York: Agathon.

Moffett, James. 1968. *Teaching the Universe of Discourse.* Boston: Houghton Mifflin Company.

Neill, Alexander S. 1960. *Summerhill.* New York: Hart Publishing Company.

Piaget, Jean. 1954. *The Construction of Reality in the Child.* New York: Basic Books, Inc.

———. 1971. *The Psychology of Intelligence.* Totowa, NJ: Littlefield Adams.

Powell, Arthur G., Eleanor Farrar, and David K. Cohen. 1985. *The Shopping Mall High School.* Boston: Houghton Mifflin Company.

Ravitch, Diane, and Chester E. Finn, Jr. 1988. *What Do Our Seventeen-Year-Olds Know? A Report on the First National Assessment of History and Literature.* New York: Harper and Row.

Russell, Bertrand. 1926. *Education and the Good Life.* New York: Liveright.

Russell, Jeffrey Burton. 1977. *The Devil: Perceptions of Evil from Antiquity to Primitive Christianity.* New York: New American Library.

Sakharov, Andrei. 1968. *Progress, Coexistence, and Intellectual Freedom.* New York: W. W. Norton.

Solzhenitsyn, Alexander. 1974. *The Gulag Archipelago 1918–1956: An Experiment in Literary Investigation.* New York: Harper and Row.

State Education Department. Bureau of Curriculum Development. *11 Social Studies: United States History and Government Tentative Syllabus.* 1987. Albany, New York: The University of the State of New York.

———. *9–10 Social Studies: Global Studies Tentative Syllabus.* 1987. Albany, New York: The University of the State of New York.

Sternberg, R.J. 1988. *The Triarchic Mind: A New Theory of Human Intelligence.* New York: Penguin Books.

Tagore, Rabindranath. 1945. "Prayer: Gitanjali." In Benét, William Rose and Norman Cousins. *The Poetry of Freedom.* New York, New York: Random House.

Vygotsky, Lev Semenovich. 1962. trans. by Eugenia Hanfmann and Gertrude Vakar. Cambridge, MA:MIT Press.

Whimbey, Arthur, and Jack Lochhead. 1982. *Beyond Problem Solving and Comprehension: A Short Course in Analytical Reasoning.* 3rd ed. Philadelphia: Franklin Institute Press.

Zaccaria, Michael A. 1978. "The Development of Historical Thinking: Implications for the Teaching of History." *The History Teacher* XI: 323–340.